Multilingual Education under Scrutiny

Esther Nieto Moreno de Diezmas /
Magdalena Custodio Espinar

Multilingual Education under Scrutiny

A Critical Analysis on CLIL Implementation and Research on a Global Scale

PETER LANG

Bibliographic Information published by the Deutsche Nationalbibliothek
The Deutsche Nationalbibliothek lists this publication in the
Deutsche Nationalbibliografie; detailed bibliographic data
is available online at http://dnb.d-nb.de.

Library of Congress Cataloging-in-Publication Data
A CIP catalog record for this book has been applied for at
the Library of Congress.

ISBN 978-3-631-87322-9 (Print)
E-ISBN 978-3-631-88361-7 (E-PDF)
E-ISBN 978-3-631-88362-4 (EPUB)
DOI 10.3726/b20079

© Peter Lang GmbH
Internationaler Verlag der Wissenschaften
Berlin 2022
All rights reserved.

Peter Lang – Berlin · Bruxelles · Lausanne · New York · Oxford

This publication has been peer reviewed.

www.peterlang.com

Dedication

To our families, for their priceless support and patience during the process of writing the present monography.

We also would like to dedicate this book to researchers, teachers and families who have devoted their efforts to underpin, implement and promote multilingualism in their respective fields of endeavour.

Foreword

Pedagogical innovations require time to take root and come to fruition – as many as 20 years, according to certain experts (Hughes, 2010). This has been the case of what is considered the most important innovation in language teaching in the last 25 years: Content and Language Integrated Learning (CLIL). From a fledgling approach to help counter Europe's deficient language levels (Pérez Cañado, 2012), it has grown exponentially, branching out in exciting new directions and spilling over into variegated realms. The ramifications of CLIL are so varied and profuse and the body of research tapping into its effects is so far-reaching and prolific that it is hugely challenging to stay abreast of its rapid evolution and to fully grasp its manifold dimensions.

This is precisely where the present monograph comes in. It provides a masterful and comprehensive overview of the past, present, and future of CLIL implementation, research, and training, creating a critical lens through which to approximate the achievements, challenges, and new directions shaping the multilingual education agenda. The authors, who are well-acknowledged voices in the field, undertake this complex task with savvy by following a three-pronged structure which touches upon all the main pillars of CLIL as a global phenomenon: its characterisation; its impact on L1, L2, and content learning; and pre- and in-service teacher education for CLIL.

The first main section crucially anchors CLIL in the European policies which led to its inception and subsequently charts its growth as an international phenomenon, which is explored from a comparative transnational perspective (Spain, Japan, and the US) and through the angle of the pluriliteracies approach. The second chief heading then proceeds to examine the complex interplay of L1, L2, and content achievement in CLIL programs by canvassing the most relevant stalwart empirical evidence on the effects of CLIL, while concomitantly identifying interesting new avenues for future research. Finally, the third thematic block taps into yet another burning issue on the CLIL scenario, namely, pre- and in-service teacher education. A systematic review of policy documents, theoretical frameworks, and practical actions is conducted, once again offering transnational research outcomes and promoting the sharing of best practices across diverse contexts.

In this sense, the distinctiveness and novelty of the present volume hinge on five main fronts. To begin with, it offers an exhaustive and well-grounded state-of-the-art of the latest specialised literature on Content and Language Integrated

Learning. This is in and of itself one of the major contributions of the monograph, given the almost infinite amount of publications which exist on the topic and which are carefully selected here for their relevance and robustness. The authors' kaleidoscopic vision and capacity to foreground the most pertinent literature are extraordinary. And this systematic review is furthermore carried out by extracting the most relevant take-aways for the reader through an insightful critical reading. What is more, the volume also maps out future pathways for progression which affect all the key issues on the current CLIL agenda, including the pluriliteracies approach, attention to diversity, translanguaging, or the integration of language and content. A fourth key asset of the monograph is its onus on the supranational perspective. This is precisely what many experts consider future research should promote (Macaro et al., 2018) and it is artfully favoured by the authors through their intercontinental perspective. Finally, and in line with the foregoing, new research outcomes are also presented via multivariate analyses and comparative studies which inform best practices from diverse contexts, which are equally showcased, crucially contributing to pushing the field forward.

For all these reasons, the far-reaching impact of the present publication ripples out through absolutely all educational levels and frontline stakeholders in the CLIL arena. It is paramount for graduates and undergraduates seeking to acquaint themselves with the basics of CLIL from a scientific and updated standpoint. It becomes crucial for teacher trainers looking to determine the content of pre- and in-service education initiatives. It is a cornerstone for researchers who want to engage in relevant investigations on truly hot topics in the field. And it is incumbent on gatekeepers and educational authorities to leverage the updated information it includes to enact research-responsive pedagogical decisions.

All in all, this is a capstone publication which provides an accomplished and realistic snapshot of where we started, where we stand, and where we need to go in the CLIL arena. The explosion of interest in CLIL implementation and research has been so outstanding that it is oftentimes difficult for those invested in the multilingual education enterprise to stay abreast of its full implications. The present publication deftly accomplishes this no meager feat. Sometimes, as they say in French, *il faut reculer pour mieux sauter*. In order to appraise the full extent of such a global and multifaceted phenomenon as CLIL, we need to stop and take a step back in order to acquire the impulse that gets us through the finish line. And this impulse is precisely what the present monograph provides by so adroitly canvassing the past, present, and future of multilingual education. A must-read tour de force for anyone interested in the development, training, and research of quality CLIL implementation.

María Luisa Pérez Cañado

References

Hughes, S. (2010). The effectiveness of bilingual education: A case study. *Paper presented at the 25th GRETA convention: Celebrating 25 years of teacher inspiration*. University of Granada.

Macaro, E., Curle, S., Pun, J., An, J., & Dearden, J. (2018). A systematic review of English medium instruction in higher education. *Language Teaching, 51*(1), 36–76.

Pérez Cañado, M. L. (2012). CLIL research in Europe: Past, present, and future. *International Journal of Bilingual Education and Bilingualism, 15*(3), 315–341.

Acknowledgement

This monograph is part of the work carried out within the research group "DiLeAr" (University of Castilla-La Mancha), and the R+D projects funded by the Spanish Ministry of Economy and Competitiveness ADiBE (grant ref. RTI2018-093390-B-I00) and ENIFALPO (grant ref. PID2019-106710GB-I00).

Multilingual education under scrutiny: A critical analysis on CLIL implementation and research on a global scale

Table of Contents

Part I. CLIL as a global trend

Chapter 1. An international review of multilingual education: CLIL across continents

Abstract: The introduction of Content and Language Integrated Learning (CLIL) in European classrooms at the end of the 20th century and its spread beyond its borders in the second decade of the 21st century constitute a complex educational phenomenon that has not been without difficulties, challenges and questions that remain to be answered. Despite its origins, linked to economic, social and linguistic policies envisaged by the European Commission, CLIL has gone beyond the European Union and has made its way into other socio-economic and political scenarios. However, while the US or Canada have the need to develop policies based on the promotion of a multicultural and multilingual education and the European Union pursues the desire to promote the use of multiple languages among their citizens, Asian countries, such as Japan, look at CLIL through pedagogical lens as an alternative to traditional English as a Foreign Language (EFL) methods (Ikeda et al., 2021). This chapter, firstly, describes the witty strategy led by the European Commission in order to increase the number of foreign languages learnt at European schools and, hence, the number of plurilingual citizens all around the EU. This ambitious policy, supported in part by the CLIL approach, has resulted in the introduction of foreign languages as the languages of instruction in mainstream education in the EU countries. Moreover, in order to grasp worldwide CLIL trends, the chapter analyses different scenarios in which this approach has anchored its theoretical foundations and principles due to its alluring nature likely to cater for the idiosyncrasies of different educational policies and institutional purposes that promote the learning of foreign languages or second and third languages through CLIL. The chapter also offers the contextualisation and analysis of the different factors influencing CLIL implementation in those scenarios. Finally, a comparative study of Spain, Japan and US is conducted to outstand how alike and different these versions of CLIL are.

Keywords: European Union, educational policy, bilingual education, multilingualism, language instruction, foreign languages.

1.1. European CLIL

Education in Europe has gone through many stages and models. This evolution is especially noteworthy in the teaching and learning of languages. At the end of the 20th century, there was an important change in the educational paradigm, promoted by the European institutions, from a linear educational model, which supported a type of education based on the intellectual culture of the Enlightenment, suitable for the industrial society, to a school capable of facing the challenges of the generation gap opened by the speed of changes in the economic, cultural and personal spheres throughout the world.

The paradigm shift has introduced an education model focused on understanding and attention to contextual and individual differences in substitution of a model focused on standards and objective knowledge of hierarchically organised subjects. This new perspective has also modified the teaching and learning of foreign and second languages, which have undergone an important transformation process. There has been a shift from methods focused almost exclusively on grammar and translation, to more eclectic approaches aimed at developing communicative competence in the second language (van Esch & St John, 2003 cited in Coyle et al., 2010). According to Jacobs and Farrell (2001), these changes in second language education can be summarised in eight: "learner autonomy, cooperative learning, curricular integration, focus on meaning, diversity, thinking skills, alternative assessment and teachers as co-learners" (p. 4). They clearly reflect the transition from positivism to post-positivism and from behaviourism to cognitivism.

However, this constructivist approach to language learning has not been fully installed in the classroom. Sometimes it has been introduced gradually, through small innovations in the school (Casanova, 2009) and, in other cases, indirectly, through the development of educational policies that include a constructivist methodology, as is the case of the Bilingual Programmes and the CLIL approach implemented all over Europe. In this vein, critical voices, such as Dendrinos', are demanding this new didactic paradigm for language education "in Europe and beyond because in today's interconnected world, the ability to speak multiple languages and communicate across linguistic devices are critical competences" (p. 9).

This new paradigm for language education, which is drawn unevenly throughout the European territory (European Commission, 2017; Dendrinos, 2018), not only affects the teaching of second or foreign languages, but it also covers the teaching of the many languages spoken in the continent (European Education and Culture Executive Agency, 2019). Furthermore, this is a change that is happening now (Marsh, 2013). To better understand the interest of the European Union in improving language learning methodologies and standards, Fig. 1 shows a selection of milestones of the language policy (1994 to present) in the EU throughout the last decades.

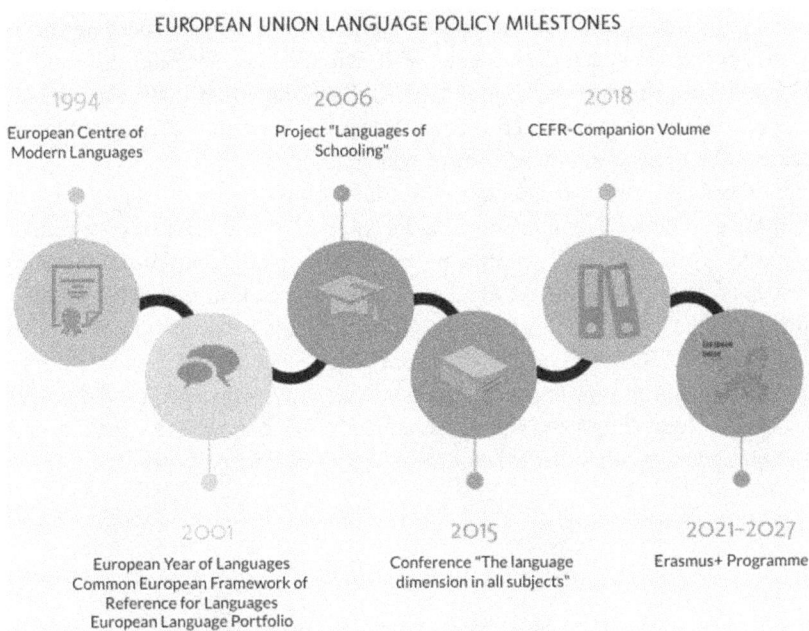

Fig.1: Timeline of the milestones in the language education policy of the EU.
Source: own elaboration, based on Council of Europe (2022)

In the course of this educational language policy, the conceptual difference between multilingual, referred to a geographical area, and plurilingual, referred to people, introduced in the Common European Framework of Reference for Languages (CEFR) (Council of Europe, 2001), deserves special attention.

> (Plurilingualism is) the ability to use languages for the purposes of communication and to take part in intercultural interaction, where a person, viewed as a social agent, has proficiency of varying degrees, in several languages, and experience of several cultures. This is not seen as the superposition or juxtaposition of distinct competences, but rather as the existence of a complex or even composite competence on which the user may draw. (Council of Europe, 2001, p. 168)

From this definition it is understood that the goal of language learning is not to acquire native-like proficiency but to be competent and be able to communicate and interact in intercultural contexts. Thus, in multilingual areas, some individuals may be monolingual, while others may be plurilingual. That is, the individuals can develop a pluricultural and intercultural competence since they are social agents in a certain context, in which they interact with different languages and cultures from which they create their own meaning. The "CEFR-Companion volume" (Council of Europe, 2018) takes account of this competence and introduces descriptors for mediation and linguistic and non-linguistic resources.

Another important instrument to assist education systems and policies in Europe is Eurydice[1], a network of 40 national units based in 37 countries of the Erasmus+ programme[2]. Its first publication to promote the implementation of CLIL across European schools was "Content and Language Integrated Learning (CLIL) at school in Europe" (European Commission, 2006). Another important publication was the "2017 Edition of Key Data on Teaching Languages at School in Europe", which pictured the education policies for teaching and learning languages in 42 European education systems (European Commission, 2017). Fig. 2 shows the versatility of the approach to work with different languages in different linguistic contexts.

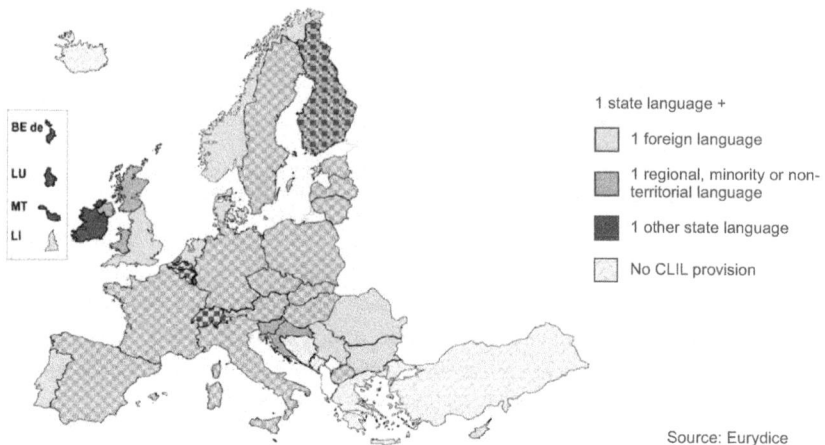

1 state language +

    1 foreign language

    1 regional, minority or non-territorial language

    1 other state language

    No CLIL provision

Source: Eurydice

Fig. 2: Status of target languages taught through CLIL in primary and/or general secondary education (ISCED 1-3), 2015/16. Source: European Commission (2017, p. 56)

1   https://eacea.ec.europa.eu/national-policies/eurydice/index_en.php_en
2   https://erasmus-plus.ec.europa.eu/

In this context, in which the starting age of the second foreign language has been advanced in a large number of European countries, one of the European Commission's priorities in linguistic matters is to help these countries to develop new pedagogical tools to guarantee that students have better learning experiences, capable of generating greater linguistic competence when they finish school. To this end, policies to reward innovation in language teaching and learning have been proposed, as well as initiatives to monitor its evolution, in collaboration with the Council of Europe and its European Centre for Modern Languages (ECML)[3], an organism launched with the main goal of introducing innovation in language teaching.

Despite the innovative character of CLIL in current education, it is important to remark that using a foreign language for teaching academic content is not new. Bilingual education has a long history, from Ancient Rome, where children were educated in Greek, to the many examples developed in the 20th century in countries where more than one language is spoken such as Luxembourg, Canada, Finland, Ireland or USA (Fernández Fontecha, 2001; Mehisto et al., 2008). Actually, CLIL has been used in border regions and areas in which the multilingual reality has demanded the learning of more than one language (Mehisto et al., 2008) years before the conceptualisation of CLIL. Thereby its novelty lies in its rapid expansion throughout Europe and the implementation and regulation of CLIL in the educational systems of many different EU countries. From the academic point of view, the works by Mohan (1986, 1991), Brinton et al. (1989) or Snow (1990), in bilingual contexts in North America, and Fruhauf et al. (1996) or Marsh and Langé (1999), in non-bilingual contexts in Europe, are clear examples of proposals that introduced the relationship between language and content in the learning of second languages before the conceptualisation and implementation of CLIL by European institutions, among which the ECML has played a key role.

The Council of Europe's ECML is an instrument to promote collaboration between researchers, experts, teachers and administrations. This centre has been promoting innovative approaches in the field of language teaching since 1995 and helping to develop and disseminate examples of good practice ever since. In the communication entitled "Promoting Language Learning and Linguistic Diversity: An Action Plan 2004-2006", it is mentioned that "content and language integrated learning (CLIL), whereby students study a subject in a foreign

---

3 https://www.ecml.at/

language, can contribute considerably to the learning objectives of the Union" (European Commission, 2006, p. 9).

Since then, the ECML has developed numerous actions and activities to promote language education across Europe, which are derived from nine key areas. As can be seen in Fig. 3, CLIL is one important thematic area of the ECML.

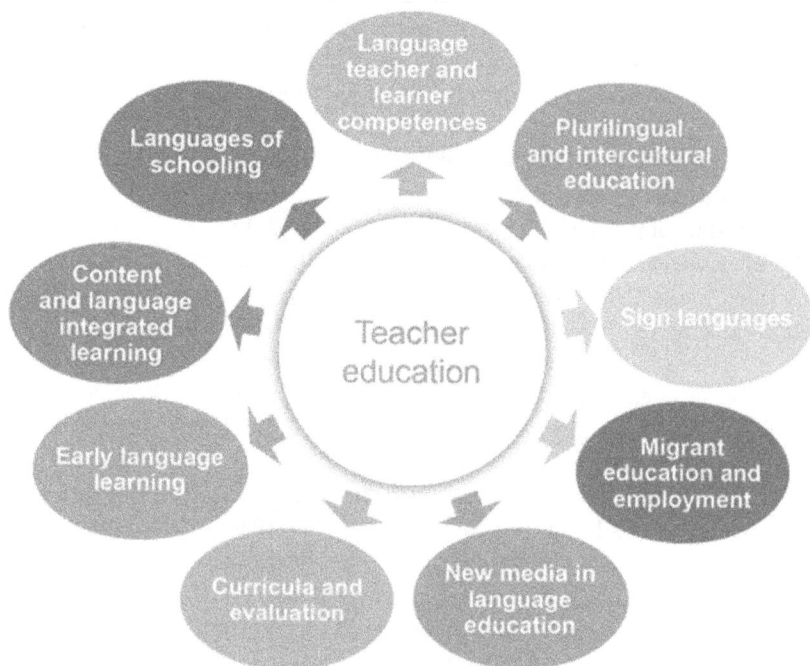

Fig. 3: Thematic areas of ECML expertise. Source: Council of Europe (ECML/CELV) (2022). https://www.ecml.at/Thematicareas/Thematicareas-Overview/tabid/1763/langu age/en-GB/Default.aspx

The future of language education in Europe is clearly oriented to keep on fostering the potential linguistic diversity of the EU and promoting the development of multilingual competences (European Commission, 2020). The EU Council Recommendation on a comprehensive approach to the teaching and learning of languages (adopted in May 2019) constitutes the framework for the development of innovative policies and practices in language teaching, among which CLIL is key to an effective application of an inclusive perspective of all languages both in education and in society. The recent publication "The future of language education in Europe: case studies of innovative practices" (European Commission, 2020) explores emerging innovative approaches and strategies of language teaching in Europe supporting learners' plurilingualism and points out eight projects and tools from the Council of Europe's ECML, which are focused on promoting plurilingual pedagogies:

- Language in subjects – Developing language awareness in subject classes (ww. ecml.at/languageinsubjects)
- A roadmap for schools to support the language(s) of schooling (www.ecml.at/roadmapforschools)
- ICT-rev – Inventory of ICT tools and open educational resources (https://ict-rev.ecml.at/)
- CONBAT+ – Plurilingualism and pluriculturalism in content-based teaching: A training kit (https://conbat.ecml.at/)
- CARAP – FREPA: A Framework of reference for pluralistic approaches to languages and cultures – Competences and resources (https://carap.ecml.at/)
- Maledive – Teaching the language of schooling in the context of diversity – Study materials for teacher development (https://maledive.ecml.at/)
- MARILLE – Promoting plurilingualism – Majority language in multilingual settings (https://marille.ecml.at/)
- CLIL-CD – European Framework for CLIL Teacher Education (https://clil-cd.ecml.at)

Other interesting websites promoted by international, national and regional institutions and individuals are:

- CLIL Cascade Network website www.ccn-clil.eu
- Onestopclil – The Resource Bank for CLIL Teachers http://www.onestopclil.com
- CoBaLTT http://www.carla.umn.edu/cobaltt/
- CAL Foreign Language http://www.cal.org/topics/fl/
- Board of Education, Valencia http://www.edu.gva.es
- MEB WEB http://www.juntadeandalucia.es/
- Department of Education, Catalonia https://web.gencat.cat/en/temes/educacio/
- GIPUZTIK http://www.gipuztik.net/ingelesa/
- EMILANGUES www.emilangues.education.fr
- Français Dans Le Monde www.fdlm.org
- Teaching English www.teachingenglish.org.uk

- CLIL/AICLE – http://www.isabelperez.com/clil.htm#arti

All these resources are intended to help European teachers and teacher educators, education administrators, curriculum developers, authors and publishers and certification authorities to face the challenges of the new emerging educational models based on CLIL.

1.2. CLIL beyond the European Union

Although CLIL is known as a European approach to language teaching, French immersion programmes in Canada and bilingual movements in the USA are told to have been a starting point or inspiration for CLIL. The controversy about the conceptualisation and definition of CLIL as a specific, well-defined pedagogical approach presented in Cenoz et al. (2013) and responded by Dalton-Puffer et al. (2014) is an evidence of the difficulty of nailing down the uniqueness of CLIL with regard to other bilingual education forms such as CBLT (Content-Based Language Teaching) or immersion. The truth is that, in a relatively short time, CLIL has resulted in an international phenomenon developed almost simultaneously in different continents and countries. After almost three decades of implementation and profuse research in Europe, CLIL has proved to be beneficial for providing bilingual education in non-bilingual communities. This fact has attracted the attention of Latin American and Asian countries (Morton, 2019), which has increased the controversy around its definition and interpretations in practice.

For example, in Latin American countries CLIL is "envisaged as a meaningful and innovative bilingual education approach in different contexts and with different learners, sometimes in connection with other L2 learning approaches, such as task-based learning (e.g., Castro García; 2017; Cendoya & Di Bin, 2010), immersion (e.g., García-Herreros Machado, 2017), or ESP (e.g., Banegas, 2018; Rojas Gonzáles & Liviero, 2014)" (Banegas et al., 2020, p. 293). Other forms of CLIL can be found in Asian countries "such as Japan, Hong Kong, Taiwan and Malaysia. However, although the label 'CLIL' is used, what is actually happening on the ground can enormously vary across contexts" (Morton, 2019, p. 5). According to the author, the CLIL developed in Asian contexts is as varied as the European one. He signals how the label "CLIL" is used differently across contexts such as Hong Kong, where it is considered an approach to content and language integration in the teaching of academic subjects, or Japan, where it consists in introducing content in language lessons (Morton, 2019, p. 5). This "soft version of CLIL" is well described by Ikeda et al. (2019). The authors suggest that in the case of Japan, where "English proficiency is important, and indeed perhaps even a requirement, and yet the language has generally been treated as a subject with sparse occasion for learners to actually use the language for communicative purposes outside the classroom" (Ikeda et al, 2021, p. 1), CLIL is seen from the eyes of EFL (English as a Foreign Language) and ELT (English Language Teaching) to address this situation and, therefore, with emphasis on language learning.

The USA and Canada are contexts with longer tradition in providing bilingual education. The difference between bilingual education provided in Europe, Asia or Latin America and that provided in these countries is that it has been developed as a necessary component of their mainstream education systems. In the USA, bilingual education has been developed to support a multilingual context derived from migration factors (Gándara & Escamilla, 2017; García, 2011). In the work by Padilla et al. (1990), the authors state their commitment "to assisting in the development of language-competent American society" (p. 7). This development includes opportunities for: (1) English-speaking individuals to develop a second (foreign language); and (2) non-native speakers of English to develop proficiency in their mother tongue.

In Canada bilingual education has been introduced to implement official policies on bilingualism and multiculturalism rooted in the development toward official bilingualism in French and English, in particular French immersion programmes, whose success has led to the development of other types of bilingual education programmes that tend to follow an immersion model (Dicks & Geneese, 2017). As pointed out by the authors, "immersion programs are a popular and generally successful option in public education that serve a variety of educational and community goals and an ever-expanding variety of students and communities in Canada" (p. 12).

Cenoz et al. (2013) affirm that "immersion programs are among the most widespread bi-multilingual education programs, not only in North America but possibly around the world" (p. 247). The same authors describe immersion as "an educational program in which an L2 or a foreign language is used for academic instruction" (p. 248). Despite the differences between CLIL and immersion argued by different European authors (Marsh, 2002; Coyle, 2007; Ball & Lyndsay, 2010; Pérez-Cañado, 2012), it is certainly difficult to describe single unique characteristics of CLIL in contrast with immersion education or CBLT. For this reason, Cenoz et al. (2013) propose that if CLIL is considered an umbrella term, immersion education can be a type of CLIL. From a different viewpoint, Dale and Tanner (2012) illustrate the relationship between CLIL and other types of bilingual education in a continuum that considers bilingual education as any form between Content-Based Language Teaching (CBLT) and immersion including all forms of CLIL in the middle of the continuum (p. 4–5). All in all, Garcia (2009) wisely states that CLIL represents a type of bilingual education that is dynamic and heteroglossic, which allows collecting all these forms of CLIL across continents.

1.3 Influencing factors in CLIL implementation at the international level

There are many reasons that have contributed to the development of CLIL as an effective approach to language teaching and learning across Europe. Firstly, it facilitates the increase of hours devoted to languages at schools without significant changes in their timetables, thus, making more efficient use of the time. Secondly, it promotes the introduction of standardised examinations connected to the CEFR (Council of Europe, 2001, 2020) and the accreditation of the language level, which is useful in terms of employment and university entrance. Thirdly, CLIL promotes pluriliteracies' development and contributes to a wider progression in language competence, including pragmatic and sociolinguistic competences, and in cognitive development, due to the intellectual demand inherent in proper CLIL lessons. Therefore, CLIL is fully aligned with the European language policy as a response to a triple socioeconomic, linguistic and cultural challenge posed by the multilingual reality and the linguistic diversity of the EU because, in addition to foreign languages, regional or minority languages are widely taught through CLIL in Europe (European Commission, 2017, p. 55). European CLIL top-down implementation through institutional policies at international, national and regional levels is, as Marsh (2002) stated, "a pragmatic European solution to a European need" (p. 11).

In line with this top-down model, bilingual education in North American countries (USA and Canada) has been introduced through governmental policies. As Gándara and Escamilla (2017) put it: "the history of bilingual education in the United States has shifted between tolerance and repression depending on politics, the economy, and the size of the immigrant population" (pp. 4–5). According to the authors, more than 60 million people use another language at home, being Spanish speakers two-thirds of this population and Chinese, French, Tagalog, Vietnamese, and Korean the next more popular. However, bilingual education remains focused on providing effective instructional practices for English language learners (ELL) who have limited English proficiency (LEP) (Moughamian et al., 2009), rather than offering actual bilingual education in two languages (Gándara & Escamilla, 2009, as cited in Gándara & Escamilla, 2017). In Canada, where immersion programmes are preferred, the principles sustaining bilingual education provision are, as explained in Dicks and Geneese (2017): (1) additive bilingualism – the assumption that acquisition of a second language brings personal, social, cognitive and economic advantage without negative effects on first language or academic development, and (2) learning a language when it is used as a medium of general curriculum instruction (in mathematics and science, for example) in an intensive and extensive time period is effective (p. 2).

From another dimension, generally speaking, East Asian CLIL is "viewed as a means by which to articulate and implement good early foreign language learning practice" (Marsh & Hood, 2008) likely to provide a meaningful context for communicative purposes (Ikeda et al., 2021). Unlike Europe or America, East Asian countries have introduced CLIL following a bottom-up implementation in a variety of contexts, which opens "a tendency for an emerging private sector to expand which provides forms of CLIL-type provision in English across all educational sectors". The CLIL Primary East Asian Context (PEAC) research summarised in Marsh and Hood (2008) signals the "pressures in the region to upgrade English language learning levels and introduce English as partial medium of instruction" (p. 48). The case of Japan, where English has become an important priority for the maintenance of Japan's technological supremacy (Ikeda, 2013) and the development of Japan as a nation (Tsuchiya, 2019), is a clear example of this. As stated by Tsuchiya and Pérez Murillo (2015): "the notion of multilingualism is absent in the policy documents and the economic demands are emphasised in the drive to teach English as an international language" (as cited in Tsuchiya, 2019, p. 43).

Notwithstanding the evidence, all these forms of bilingual education have in common an economic factor behind their implementation that "represents languages as commodities for employability, mobility and economic growth" (Dendrinos, 2018, p. 9), and what it implies.

1.4. The crucible of CLIL

Dale and Tanner (2012) describe a useful continuum between language and content that can help to understand the different varieties of CLIL around the world. They consider that CBLT is performed by language teachers who teach a language through topics based on content. On the other side of the continuum, there is immersion, in which content teachers teach subjects in a language that is not the mother tongue of the student. CLIL, according to these authors, is between these two forms of bilingual education. Therefore, if it is closer to CBLT, then CLIL is language oriented and performed by language teachers, and if CLIL is closer to immersion programmes, then it is content oriented and imparted by content teachers (Dale & Tanner, 2012, pp. 4–5). This flexible interpretation allows a creative implementation of different models of CLIL, which is in line with Bentley's descriptions of two main models: soft CLIL and hard CLIL. This continuum allows the implementation of variants more or less language-led, content-led, including partial immersion forms of bilingual education (Bentley, 2010; Ball et al., 2015). In Fig. 4, different models of bilingual education are displayed in the continuum according to their characteristics.

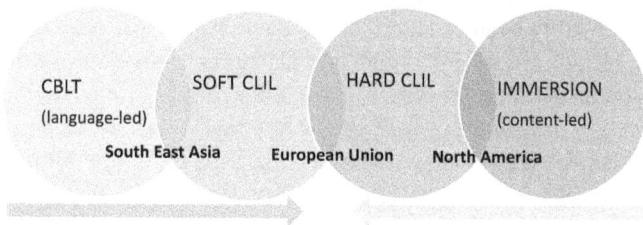

Fig. 4: Bilingual education continuum from an international perspective. Source: own elaboration

According to this diagram, Japanese soft CLIL described in Ikeda (2021) is a clear example of the attempt to move from traditional English language teaching (ELT) to a more contextualised and authentic use of the foreign language in the classroom. A good example to illustrate different types of CLIL, including soft and hard versions, is Spain, which has become one of the benchmarks in Europe in the development of bilingual and multilingual educational policies based on CLIL (Megías, 2012; Coyle et al., 2010). The rich and diverse Spanish linguistic educational panorama is shown in Tab. 1.

Tab. 1: Languages of instruction in the Spanish education system

Status	Languages of instruction	Levels
Official language + Foreign language	Spanish + English/French/German/Italian/Portuguese	P S B

Official language + Regional official language	Spanish + Basque/Catalan/Galician/Oc- citan/Valencian	P S B
Official language + Regional official language + Foreign language	Spanish + Basque + English/French Spanish + Catalan + English/French Spanish + Galician + English/French/ Italian/Portuguese Spanish + Valencian + English/French/ Italian/Portuguese	P S B
	Spanish + Catalan + Portuguese	S B

*Primary, Secondary and Bachillerato (Higher Secondary Education). *Source:* adapted from European Commission (2017, p. 161)

Finally, Dicks and Geneese (2017) describe the following types of immersion in Canada:

(1) French immersion (FI), originally mainly for English-speaking majority students, but now also populated by learners from non-official minority language backgrounds (Taylor, 2010), (2) heritage language (HL) programs for students with backgrounds in non-official languages such as Ukrainian, German, and Mandarin, and (3) indigenous language programs for aboriginal students (e.g., students of Inuit, Mohawk or Cree backgrounds) (pp. 1–2)

These varied examples of bilingual education provision demonstrate CLIL's melting pot and, beyond the problems of its definition and conceptualisation, it is clear that CLIL is an approach to language teaching in line with current sociolinguistic and socioeconomic demands around the world.

Bibliography

Ball, P., & Lindsay, D. (2010). Teacher training for CLIL in the Basque Country: The case of the Ikastolas-An expediency model. In D. Lasagabaster & Y. Ruiz de Zarobe (Eds.), *CLIL in Spain: Implementation, results and teacher training* (pp. 162–187). Cambridge Scholars Publishing.

Ball, P., Kelly, K., & Clegg, J. (2015). *Putting CLIL into practice*. Oxford University Press.

Banegas, D. L., Poole, P., & Corrales, K. (2020). Content and language integrated learning in Latin America 2008–2018: Ten years of research and practice. *Studies in Second Language Learning & Teaching, 10*(2), 283–305.

Bentley, K. (2010). *The TKT (Teaching Knowledge Test) course. CLIL module content and language integrated learning.* Cambridge University Press.

Brinton, D. M., Snow, M. A., & Wesche, M. B. (1989). *Content-based second language instruction.* Heinle and Heinle Publishers.

Casanova, M. A. (2009). *Diseño curricular e innovación educativa.* La Muralla S.A.

Comunidad de Madrid (2020). *Datos y cifras de la educación 2020-21.* Consejería de Educación, Juventud y Deporte. https://www.comunidad.madrid/servic ios/educacion/educacion-cifras

Council of Europe. (2001). *Common European framework of reference for languages: Learning, teaching, assessment.* Cambridge University Press.

Council of Europe. (2020). *Common European framework of reference for languages: Learning, teaching, assessment – Companion volume.* Council of Europe Publishing. www.coe.int/lang-cefr

Council of Europe. (2022, February). *Language police. Milestones.* Council of Europe portal. https://www.coe.int/en/web/language-policy/milestones

Council of Europe (ECML/CELV). (2022, February). *Thematic areas of ECML expertise.* https://www.ecml.at/Thematicareas/Thematicareas-Overview/ tabid/1763/language/en-GB/Default.aspx

Coyle, D. (2007). Towards a connected research agenda for CLIL pedagogies. *The International Journal of Bilingual Education and Bilingualism, 10,* 543–62.

Coyle, D., Hood, P., & Marsh, D. (2010). *CLIL – Content and language integrated learning.* Cambridge University Press.

Dale, L., & Tanner, R. (2012). *CLIL activities. A resource for subject and language teachers.* Cambridge University Press.

Dalton-Puffer, C., Llinares, A., Lorenzo, F., & Nikula, T. (2014). "You can stand under my umbrella": Immersion, CLIL and bilingual education. A response to Cenoz, Genesee & Gorter (2013). *Applied Linguistics, 35*(2), 213–218.

Dendrinos, B. (2018). Multilingualism language policy in the EU today: A paradigm shift in language education. *Training, Language and Culture, 2*(3), 9–28. https://doi.org/10.29366/2018tlc.2.3.1

Dicks, J., & Genesee, F. (2017). Bilingual education in Canada. In O. Garcia, A. Lin, & S. May (Eds.), *Encyclopedia of language and education. Bilingual and multilingual education* (3rd ed., pp. 453–467). Springer, Cham. https://doi. org/10.1007/978-3-319-02324-3_32-1

European Commission, Directorate-General for Education, Youth, Sport and Culture. (2006). *Content and language integrated learning (CLIL) at school in Europe.* Publications Office.

European Commission, Directorate-General for Education, Youth, Sport and Culture, Szőnyi, E., Siarova, H., & Le Pichon-Vorstman, E. (2020). *The future of language education in Europe: Case studies of innovative practices: Executive summary*. Publications Office. https://data.europa.eu/doi/10.2766/81169

European Commission/EACEA/Eurydice. (2017). *Key data on teaching languages at school in Europe – 2017 edition. Eurydice report*. Publications Office.

European Education and Culture Executive Agency, Eurydice, Baïdak, N., & Noorani, S. (2019). *The teaching of regional and minority languages in schools in Europe*. Publications Office. https://data.europa.eu/doi/10.2797/688166

Fernández Fontecha, A. (2001). Una revisión bibliográfica sobre el método AICLE (aprendizaje integrado de contenidos curriculares y lengua extranjera). *Contextos Educativos, 4*, 217–239. https://doi.org/10.18172/con.494

Fruhauf, G., Coyle, D., & Christ, I. (Eds.). (1996). *Teaching content in a foreign language: Practice and perspectives in European bilingual education*. Stichting Europees Platform voor het Nederlandse Onderwjis.

Gándara, P., & Escamilla, K. (2017). Bilingual education in the United States. *Bilingual and Multilingual Education, 12*, 439–452.

García, O. (2011). *Bilingual education in the 21st century: A global perspective*. John Wiley & Sons.

Ikeda, M., Izumi, S., Watanabe, Y., Pinner, R., & Davis, M. (2021). *Soft CLIL and English language teaching: Understanding Japanese policy, practice and implications*. Routledge.

Jacobs, G. M., & Farrell, T. S. C. (2001). Paradigm shift: Understanding and implementing change in second language education. *TESL-EJ, 5*(1), 1–17.

Marsh, D. (Ed.). (2002). *CLIL/EMILE the European dimension*. University of Jyväskyla.

Marsh, D. (2013). *The CLIL trajectory: Educational innovation for the 21st century generation*. Servicio de Publicaciones de la Universidad de Córdoba.

Marsh, D., & Hood, P. (March, 2008). Content and language integrated learning in primary East Asia contexts (CLIL PEAC). In *The proceedings of the primary innovations regional seminar* (pp. 43–50).

Marsh, D., & Langé, G. (Eds.). (1999) *Implementing content and language integrated learning*. University of Jyväskylä.

Megías Rosa, M. (2012). Formación, Integración y colaboración: Palabras clave de CLIL. Una Charla con María Jesús Frigols. *Encuentro, 21*, 3–14.

Mehisto, P., Marsh, D., & Frigols, M. J. (2008). *Uncovering CLIL: Content and language integrated learning in bilingual and multilingual education*. Macmillan Education.

Mohan, B. A. (1986). *Language and content.* Addison-Wesley.

Mohan, B. A. (1991). LEP students and the integration of language and content: Knowledge structures and tasks. In A. Stein (Ed.), *National research symposium on LEP students' issues.* U.S. Department of Education, Office of Bilingual Education Research and Evaluation.

Morton, T. (2019). Foreword: CLIL as transgressive policy and practice. In T. Keiko & M. D. Pérez-Murillo (Eds.), *Content and language integrated learning in Spanish and Japanese context. Policy, practice and pedagogy* (1st ed., pp. 5–12). Cham: Palgrave Macmillan

Moughamian, A. C., Rivera, M. O., & Francis, D. J. (2009). *Instructional models and strategies for teaching English language learners.* Center on Instruction; University of Houston, Texas Institute for Measurement, Evaluation, and Statistics. Retrieved February 8, 2022, from https://eric.ed.gov/?id=ED517794

Padilla, A. M., Fairchild, H. H., & Valadez, C. M. (Eds.). (1990). *Foreign language education: Issues and strategies* (Vol. 113). Sage Publications.

Pérez-Cañado, M. L. (2012). CLIL research in Europe: Past, present, and future. *International Journal of Bilingual Education and Bilingualism, 15,* 315–41.

Snow, M. A. (1990). Language immersion: An overview and comparison. In A. M. Padilla, H. H. Fairchild, & C. M. Valadez (Eds.), *Foreign language education: Issues and strategies.* Sage Publications.

Tsuchiya, K. (2019). CLIL and language education in Japan. In K. Tsuchiya & M.D. Pérez Murillo (Eds.), *Content and language integrated learning in Spanish and Japanese contexts* (pp. 37–56). Cham: Palgrave Macmillan. https://doi.org/10.1007/978-3-030-27443-6_3

Chapter 2. The multiple faces of CLIL

Abstract: Despite CLIL's successful journey both from a theoretical and practical point of view, there is still a wide margin of improvement to guarantee its viability and long-term sustainability in the European Union and beyond. From the first works that addressed CLIL pedagogy as a whole construct (Mehisto et al., 2008; Coyle et al., 2010; Ball et al., 2015), in recent years, CLIL works, and projects have moved towards the analysis and conceptualisation of specific areas such as evaluation (Leontjev & DeBoer, 2020) and attention to diversity (Pérez-Cañado et al., 2021) in CLIL classrooms. Moreover, the complexity of contextual implementation of CLIL across continents, which is described in this work, goes beyond the so-called "bilingual classroom", and opens the conceptualisation of CLIL towards an ecological phenomenon within the (plurilingual) education agenda (Coyle, 2018).This chapter opens the door to a new era of CLIL in which the already versatile nature of this approach faces the challenge of adapting to the needs of different social, economic and cultural contexts and anticipating the phenomena that all this entails. Therefore, the repercussions of learning through CLIL on content acquisition and language development, as well as the impact on attaining other learning outcomes such as cross-curricular competences, (inter) cultural competence, or academic performance, must be revisited from the perspective of pluriliterate CLIL learners, because subject literacies are the key to deep learning and the development of transferable skills. This must be reflected in teachers' competence to plan CLIL lessons; hence, CLIL teacher education and training are in need to anticipate these teaching skills too.

In this sense, the chapter offers a drawing of the path and implications that the original introduction of CLIL as the European approach to language learning, which has gone beyond its borders, has suffered on the educational panorama, at an international level, moving from a linguistic focus to an increasing role of CLIL as a pedagogic phenomenon, with a transformative potential (Ikeda, 2021), that is expected to play a central role in future steps in the CLIL agenda worldwide.

Keywords: Bilingual education, educational sciences, plurilingualism, foreign languages, educational models.

2.1. From the theoretical foundations of European CLIL to a multimodal approach

One of the most cited definitions of CLIL is the one provided by Coyle et al. (2010): CLIL is "a dual-focused educational approach in which an additional language is used for the learning and teaching of both content and language" (p. 1). Since then, CLIL has also been seen as "a type of instruction that fuses the best of subject matter and language teaching pedagogies" (Morton, 2010, p. 97) or, even "CLIL could be interpreted as a foreign language enrichment measure packaged into content teaching" (Dalton-Puffer, 2011, p. 184). This open eclectic nature of CLIL's methodological and pedagogical principles has made CLIL a malleable attractive approach for numerous contexts in which traditional language teaching does not offer the expected results and CLIL is sought as the means of improving linguistic skills both in monolingual and multilingual contexts (Dalton-Puffer, 2011; Ikeda et al., 2019; Wei & Feng, 2015). Pérez-Cañado (2016, p. 12) collects some references that illustrate this terminological controversy: "CLIL has been challenged for its 'ill-defined nature' (Paran, 2013, p. 318), 'convenient vagueness' (Bruton, 2013, p. 588), and 'internal ambiguity' (Cenoz et al., 2013, p. 2)". The author concludes that the focus should move from this controversy to the acknowledgement that CLIL has different formats in order to ensure that "the results and effects of all types of multilingual programmes (be they CLIL, CBI, or immersion) are shared so that the pedagogical and research community can benefit from them" (Pérez-Cañado, p. 14).

In this sense, Hemmi and Banegas (2021) portray a wide variety of CLIL models adapted to different cultural and educational contexts placed in different geographical scenarios. From a pedagogical point of view, Ikeda et al. (2019) present an interpretation of soft CLIL in Japan likely to promote the necessary paradigm shift in ELT (English Language Teaching), from traditional instruction based on positivism, in which the objective, the final result and the teacher control have prevailed, to methodologies of a constructivist nature, highly contextualised, in which the subjective, the process and student understanding occupy the central axis of the teaching and learning processes (Jacobs & Farrell, 2001), as implied by the development of CLIL in the classroom (Dalton-Puffer, 2011, p. 189). This modality of CLIL clearly exemplifies the role of CLIL as "a catalyst for change in language education" (Marsh & Frigols, 2007, p. 3). But even in Europe, there are countries where the local implementations of CLIL, due to a lack of unified CLIL policy at the national level, have resulted in "a marked gap between CLIL specialists' or policy-makers' perceptions about what CLIL pedagogies should consist of and those involved with its day-to-day implementation" (van Kampen et al., 2020, p. 856).

Outside Europe, bilingual education has also evolved. According to García and Otheguy (2020) important aspects of bilingual education such as translanguaging have been limited by "the strict language allocation policies that have accompanied the growth of dual language education programmes in the last decade in the USA, which come close to the neoliberal understanding of multilingualism espoused in the European Union" (p. 15). In line with Dalton-Puffer's (2011) definition, Wei and Feng (2015) refer to the potential of CLIL as an interesting approach beyond Europe in EFL contexts such as China and other Asian countries.

Despite the multiple variants of bilingual education, some of them implemented under the acronym of CLIL, Dalton-Puffer (2011, pp. 183–184) identifies the following main features of CLIL regardless of the geographical context:

- CLIL is about using a foreign language or a lingua franca, not a second language (L2).
- The dominant CLIL language is English, reflecting the fact that a command of English as an additional language is increasingly regarded as a key literacy feature worldwide.
- CLIL also implies that teachers will normally be non-native speakers of the target language.
- This means that CLIL lessons are usually timetabled as content lessons, while the target language normally continues as a subject in its own right in the shape of foreign language lessons taught by language specialists.
- In CLIL programmes typically less than 50% of the curriculum is taught in the target language.
- CLIL is usually implemented once learners have already acquired literacy skills in their first language (L1), which is more often at the secondary than the primary level in the European scene.

From a pedagogical perspective, according to van Kampen et al. (2020) CLIL pedagogies should include:

- The holistic 4Cs framework by Coyle (2007).
- A genre-based pedagogy that provides a way to integrate language and content (e.g., Morton, 2010).
- Effective second language pedagogy (de Graaff et al., 2007).
- Social-constructivist and interactive approach in which students are active learners (learner-centred teaching) and teachers act as facilitators of learning.

- Collaborative teaching and learning to ensure linguistic support.

CLIL sustainability lies in the development of effective content learning strategies and language acquisition opportunities based on these pedagogies. However, the alignment between perceptions of stakeholders in different contexts where CLIL is implemented with these theoretical foundations might not always occur. Particularly, Wei and Feng (2015) collect some evidence from Asian countries such as China, Vietnam or South Korea on the barriers formal CLIL policy implementation must face in those countries such as lack of understanding and support from leaders and managers, worries and complaints from teachers, parents, students and from the media, and the mismatch between stakeholders' language beliefs and formal language policy, which clearly constrains the development of CLIL.

This need for alignment with a particular understanding of CLIL is analysed by Banegas and Hemmi (2021) who assert that European CLIL should not be the norm against which experiences around the world are measured, since even in the Netherlands, where CLIL provisions are highly institutionalised at the national level, van Kampen et al. (2020) report that of these ideal pedagogies "a few aspects were either mentioned by only a minority of practitioners or were mentioned by interviewees as being difficult to practically realize. These include teaching students subject-specific discourses, providing feedback on students' language use, and collaboration between CLIL and target language teachers" (p. 868).

However, Gabillon remarks that contextual differences such as intensity, objectives, programme type, language proficiency level, age, or language of instruction "lead to curriculum variations in the implementation of CLIL, which would not influence the theoretical principles underlying the approach" (Gabillon, 2020). Thus, the multi-dimensionality, rather than multi-modality, resulting from diverse implementations of CLIL (Gabillon, 2020) should not affect what CLIL is and serve as an excuse to simplify or dilute the theoretical foundations of the CLIL approach.

Therefore, it is necessary to boost the relationship between theory (specialists in CLIL and institutions) and practice (CLIL teachers and students) since "a shared knowledge base between these stakeholders is necessary to support the systematic development of CLIL, to support teachers in learning how to teach using CLIL, and to ensure a high quality of CLIL education is sustained" (van Kampen et al., 2020, p. 868). A similar conclusion is offered by Wei and Feng (2015) when they state that "the benefits of CLIL programmes for young learners can only be maximized when people's language practices, beliefs and the authorities' management are consistent with each other" (p. 60).

Notwithstanding, Banegas and Hemmi (2021) point out that CLIL, from a global perspective, is still in need of regulations and educational policies designed to allow teachers and schools to offer quality CLIL modalities, because "if CLIL is to be adopted as an educational approach, then institutions need to accommodate multilingual practices and interculturality across almost all domains of institutional life and not just those pertaining to classroom experience" (p. 7). Besides, as Dalton-Puffer (2020) remarks, in many cases, CLIL practices are not only promoted to achieve a certain level of language proficiency, while mastering the content as if it was learnt in the L1, but to introduce additional expectations in these forms of bilingual education such as:

> deepen the degree of subject learning through cognitive stimulation; offer access to knowledge repositories available in other languages; better prepare students for a professional career in an era of globalisation; deepen intercultural understanding and language awareness; provide a more learner-centred and innovative didactic approach; overcome traditional subject boundaries, to name but a few. (Dalton-Puffer, 2020)

The author illustrates this diversity of CLIL resorting to the two types of CLIL (see Fig. 3 in Chapter 1): type A CLIL in content lessons (hard CLIL) and type B CLIL in FLT (soft CLIL), which fit the many different modalities of CLIL from an international perspective.

2.2. Beyond the 4Cs: Affective factors and attention to diversity in CLIL classrooms

2.2.1. Affective factors in CLIL: Authenticity and motivation

There are many factors around CLIL implementation and its repercussions. Chapters 3, 4 and 5 deal with the most studied ones. However, beyond the integrated learning of content and language, the cognitive development and the intercultural growth ascribed to this approach, CLIL "is a significant source for the self-confident and self-evident use of the foreign language and its ultimate appropriation by many CLIL learners, which is regularly observed to be the most striking outcome of CLIL programs" (Dalton-Puffer, 2011, p. 196). Dale and Tanner (2012) also include motivation among the many benefits of CLIL for learners. According to the authors, the rapid progress experienced by students in their additional language makes them develop a strong sense of achievement. Looking more deeply at the affective factors in language learning, Pinner (2019) traces a strong conceptual link between authenticity and motivation regarding the contents, materials and tasks chosen and designed by teachers to promote language interaction in the classroom. In the context of CLIL, quality learning materials are designed to boost intrinsic motivation (Mehisto, 2012).

Moreover, "CLIL-specific learning materials support the creation of enriched learning environments where students can simultaneously learn both content and language, whilst becoming more adept learners of both" (p. 17). Higher-order thinking skill (HOTS) development involves exploring, discussing, and meaningfully constructing concepts and relationships in the CLIL classroom. Hence, it is paramount to provide students with contexts that involve real-world problems, applications and projects that are relevant to them and can make their learning more motivating and hands-on. As stated by van Lier (1996, cited in Pinner, 2019): "an action is authentic when it realises a free choice and is an expression of what a person genuinely feels and believes. An authentic action is intrinsically motivating" (p. 6).

In addition to generating an ideal context for learning declarative (facts and concepts) and procedural content, authentic tasks facilitate the effective integration of language in the CLIL classroom. Language genres or text types can be linked to these final products to allow the explicit teaching, learning and assessment of the language in CLIL (Morton, 2010). Finally, authentic learning boosts the assessment of students' ability to effectively use their knowledge or skills to complete a task rather than their mere understanding of the content studied (Leontjev & DeBoer, 2020). This symbiotic relationship between authenticity and motivation in CLIL needs to be explored and revisited from the perspective of the new conceptualisation of motivation (Pinner, 2019). Despite the increased number of studies about motivation, there is still a lack of empirical research on the potential of these interconnected components of language learning (Pinner, 2019) in general, and in CLIL, in particular (Doiz et al., 2014), in which there is also the authenticity of purpose from the point of view of the language.

For this reason, Doiz et al. (2014) opened the door to the study of individual and contextual variables, which have little to do with CLIL, but might be affecting the claimed positive outcomes of CLIL such as the satisfaction and emotional balance for CLIL students derived from having overcome a difficult challenge (Seikkula-Leino, 2007). In this vein, Pérez-Cañado (2016) suggests the study of "four different variables: verbal intelligence, motivation (where four factors have been considered: will, anxiety, disinterest, and self-demand), socio-economic status, and extramural exposure to the foreign language to determine the homogeneity of CLIL and non-CLIL classes" (p. 19) to guarantee an accurate interpretation of empirical CLIL results.

2.2.2 Attention to diversity in CLIL

Another important aspect of CLIL concerning its sustainability is to respond to the needs demanded by educational differentiation. The idea of elitism and segregation has flown over CLIL since its origin. The works of Bruton (2011, 2013) and Paran (2013) cited in Pérez-Cañado et al. (2021) have drawn attention to this belief. However, the authors present three main findings from recent investigations that dismantle the assumption that CLIL is elitist:

> To begin with, CLIL and non-CLIL students have been found to be increasingly homogeneous in hundreds of randomly chosen schools where both types of streams co-existed. Secondly, CLIL has been found to work very successfully even in the most disenfranchised settings: in rural contexts, public schools, with low socioeconomic status (SES), and with minority ethnicities. Finally, CLIL has been found to have a leveler effect, since, while differences in terms of setting, SES, or type of school are sustained in non-bilingual groups, they phase out in CLIL branches. (p. 2)

From a different perspective, Barrios Espinosa (2019) discusses "egalitarianism" in CLIL, concluding that the lowest educated parents are the most satisfied with the bilingual programme and they show little concern about content learning even though they are aware that their children are struggling in CLIL the most. In a middle position, with respect to the phenomenon of diversity, Bauer-Marschallinger et al. (2021) suggest an ambivalence inherent in the (Austrian) system between segregation and egalitarianism.

With regard to scientific research in the field of differentiation in CLIL, Pérez-Cañado (2021) reports the results of the first cross-European comparison of stakeholder perspectives on catering to diversity within CLIL programmes. Fig. 5 shows the main positive and negative outcomes from the study that involves 59 secondary schools from six European countries (Austria, Finland, Germany, Italy, Spain, and the UK).

Proper attention
to diverstiy in CLIL

Areas to improve
for attending
diversity in CLIL

Teachers
communicative
habilities, scaffolding

Materials, summative
evaluation, teacher
training,
multiprofesional teams

ICT, formative
evaluation

Learner-centred
methodologies and
groupings,
collaboration with
language assistants

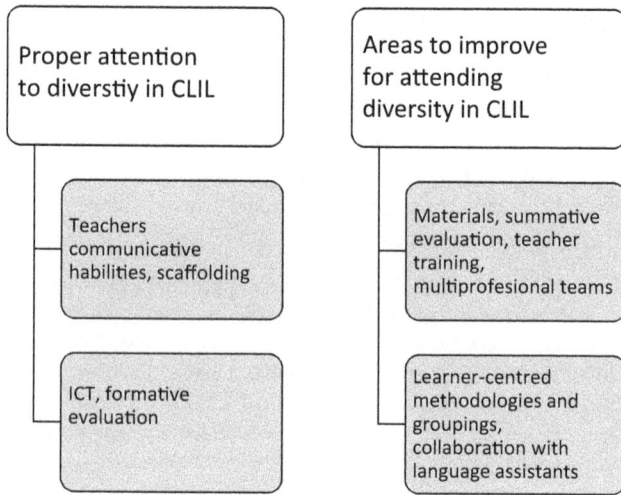

Fig. 5: Differentiation in CLIL programmes. Source: Own elaboration based on Pérez-Cañado (2021)

These areas are systematically perceived more positively by the teachers than the students and parents. From them, Pérez-Cañado highlights four key factors to effective attention to diversity:

1. The current CLIL provision, as it stands, does not fit the bill in the new main-streaming scenario
2. Different countries deal with selectivity and inclusion in very different ways, and diverse policies and practices need to be implemented to respond adequately to these variegated realities
3. The identified key areas to effectively attend diversity need to be part of future teacher development courses since teacher training is a crucial step in creating sustainable change
4. Bilingual education continues to be viewed as prestigious and worthwhile (2021, pp. 14–15)

One more time, the idea of multiple forms, realities and contexts of CLIL is reflected in the results. A very interesting contribution in this area, conceived from a bottom-up teacher-led initiative to attend multilingual, multicultural dynamic learning communities is presented by Coyle et al. (2021) as "a sustainable pedagogic evolution" (p. 2). This vision of teachers as designers is a very effective strategy to adapt CLIL provision to different realities accounting for particular contextual factors such as *point de depart*, professional learning, connected domains, diversity, combining pedagogies and learner-centredness (Coyle et al., 2021, p. 5). According to the authors, "the data provide a strong, shared, values-driven understanding of diversity by teachers and students across the entire age range" (p. 13), which allows looking at these factors as a reference to map out the strategies to improve diversity at school from the school itself.

Deepening the idea of sustainable change, Siepmann et al. (2021) remark, as Pérez-Cañado does, the need for using the findings on heterogeneity in CLIL for the creation of research-informed CLIL teaching materials and teacher-training resources, two of the areas of improvement detected to effectively attend diversity in CLIL settings.

2.3. CLIL as an ecological phenomenon

The revolution in language education that we are experiencing has brought into discussion key concepts such as polylanguaging, "which denotes the way in which speakers use features associated with different 'languages' – even when they know very little of these 'languages'" (Jørgensen, 2011, p. 23), translanguaging, understood as the "act performed by bilinguals of accessing different linguistic features or various modes of what are described as autonomous languages, in order to maximize communicative potential" (García, 2009, p. 140) and plurilingualism (see Chapter 1). Gabillon (2020) analyses the influence of postmodernist definitions of applied linguistic in the statements pronounced by CLIL experts evidencing the "unstable, unpredictable, creative and unique nature of the learning process and its variability in relation to different contexts" and explaining "the reasons for some of the characteristics of CLIL, such as the multidimensionality and variability of its implementation" (Gabillon, 2020). The author describes how CLIL has developed a "new understanding of language", under the influence of recent research in sociology, anthropology and sociolinguistics, which analyses the role of language and language use in the changing global social ecology caused by "transnationalism" (the spread and diffusion of social, political and economic movements between and across the borders of individual nation-states, Vertovec, 2009, cited in Gabillon, 2020) and "superdiversity" (a complex social, cultural, economic diversity in societies "… diversity within diversity, a tremendous increase in the texture of diversity in societies …" Blommaert, 2013, p. 4, cited in Gabillon, 2020). From this perspective, CLIL is not exclusive of bilingual education but part of the wider context of plurilingual education.

In this scenario of plurilingualism, Meyer et al. (2015) explain that "helping our students become pluriliterate (= acquiring subject literacy in more than one language) will empower them to construct and communicate knowledge purposefully and successfully across languages and cultures and prepare them for living and working in the 'knowledge age'" (p. 3). This vision of the language of CLIL opens the conceptualisation of CLIL towards an ecological phenomenon within the (plurilingual) education agenda (Coyle, 2018).

This renewed understanding of literacies development is based on five fundamental principles that need to be planned for and consciously fostered in the content subject lessons (Meyer et al., 2015). Fig. 6 shows the principles of pluriliteracies teaching for learning (PTL).

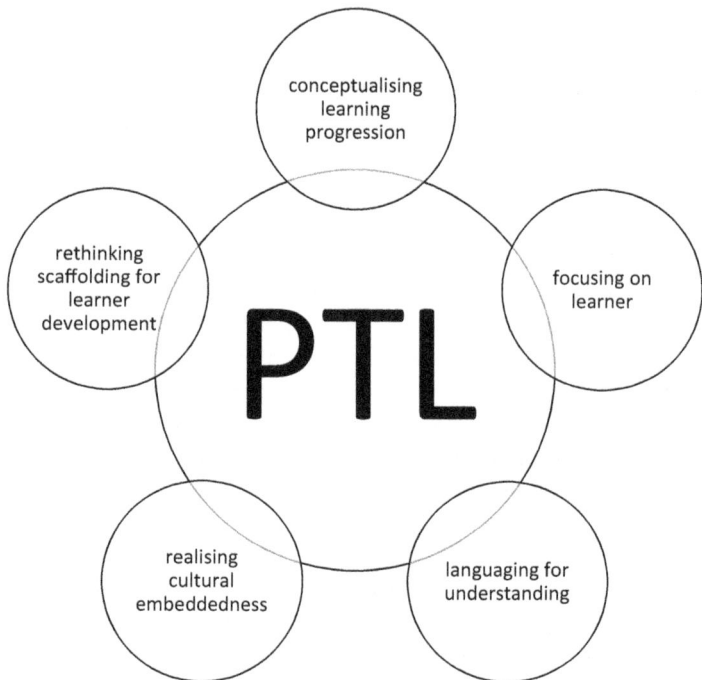

Fig. 6: The principles of pluriliteracies teaching for learning (PTL). Source: Own creation based on Meyer et al. (2015)

Among the implications of this new approach to language learning in CLIL, there is the need to look at materials and teacher's competence to plan CLIL lessons with pluriliteracies focus that successfully combine opportunities for "languaging" as a means of mediating students' thinking and understanding of content. For this, teachers are supposed to design materials and provide authentic tasks and activities linked to specific genres, which are key to the development of cognitive discourse functions (CDFs) and language (genre) awareness. The language of CLIL should be a visible component of the learning process in order to be assessed in an integrated manner. As Banegas and Hemmi (2021) put it, "in so doing, the future of CLIL preparation may be strengthened by incorporating teachers' trajectories and cognitions and help them direct their own professional development" (p. 9).

Another important implication of this plurilingual perspective is the role of other languages in the CLIL classroom. There are authors who suggest their potential to overcome the barriers for lower L2 proficiency students to engage with complex academic learning (Banegas & Hemmi, 2021). However, although the presence and benefits of translanguaging (using learner's L1, mainly in monolingual contexts) have been proved (Martínez-Adrián, 2020; Ortega, 2019; Tsuchiya, 2019), Banegas and Hemmi point out that "there is still a tendency to be suspicious" about the introduction of other languages in the CLIL classroom, which clearly contradicts the plurilingual approach to the language of CLIL by perpetuating "a monolingual idealism perspective" which, according to the authors, "denies learners the right to exercise their multilingual identities (Manan & Tul-Kubra, 2020)" (2019, p. 11).

All in all, if CLIL is to be seen as an evolving educational approach likely to adopt multiple faces, there is still a long way to revisit and redefine it through empirical observation and analysis of current CLIL practices.

Bibliography

Ball, P., Clegg, J., & Kelly, K. (2015). *Putting CLIL into practice.* Oxford University Press.

Banegas, D. L., & Hemmi, C. (2021). CLIL: Present and future. In C. Hemmi & D. L. Banegas (Eds.), *International perspectives on CLIL* (pp. 281–296). Cham: Palgrave.

Barrios Espinosa, E. (2019). The effect of parental education level on perceptions about CLIL: A study in Andalusia. *International Journal of Bilingual Education and Bilingualism*, 25(1), 183–195

Bauer-Marschallinger, S., Dalton-Puffer, C., Heaney, H., Katzinger, L., & Smit, U. (2021). CLIL for all? An exploratory study of reported pedagogical practices in Austrian secondary schools. *International Journal of Bilingual Education and Bilingualism*, 1–16. https://doi.org/10.1080/13670050.2021.1996533

Coyle, D. (2018) The place of CLIL in (Bilingual) education, *Theory Into Practice*, 57(3), 166–176. https://doi.org/10.1080/00405841.2018.1459096

Coyle, D., Bower, K., Foley, Y., & Hancock, J. (2021). Teachers as designers of learning in diverse, bilingual classrooms in England: An ADiBE case study. *International Journal of Bilingual Education and Bilingualism*, 1–19. https://doi.org/10.1080/13670050.2021.1989373

Coyle, D., Hood, P., & Marsh, D. (2010). *CLIL – Content and language integrated learning*. Cambridge University Press.

Dale, L., & Tanner, R. (2012). *CLIL activities with CD-ROM: A resource for subject and language teachers*. Cambridge University Press.

Dalton-Puffer, C. (2011). Content-and-language integrated learning: From practice to principles? *Annual Review of Applied Linguistics*, 31, 182–204.

Dalton-Puffer, C. (2020). CLIL in practice: What does the research tell us? Retrieved from https://www.goethe.de/en/spr/unt/kum/clg/20984546.html

Doiz, A., Lasagabaster, D., & Sierra, J. M. (2014). CLIL and motivation: The effect of individual and contextual variables. *The Language Learning Journal*, 42(2), 209–224. https://doi.org/10.1080/09571736.2014.889508

Gabillon, Z. (2020). Revisiting CLIL: Background, pedagogy, and theoretical underpinnings. Contextes et didactiques. *Revue semestrielle en sciences de l'éducation*, (15). https://doi.org/10.4000/ced.1836

García, O. (2009). Education, multilingualism and translanguaging in the 21st century. In T. Skutnabb-Kangas, R. Phillipson, A. K. Mohanty, & M. Panda (Eds.), *Social justice through multilingual education* (pp. 140–158). Multilingual Matters.

García, O., & Otheguy, R. (2020). Plurilingualism and translanguaging: Commonalities and divergences. *International Journal of Bilingual Education and Bilingualism*, 23(1), 17–35.

Hemmi, C., & Banegas, D. L. (Eds.). (2021). *International perspectives on CLIL*. Palgrave Macmillan.

Ikeda, M., Izumi, S., Watanabe, Y., Pinner, R., & Davis, M. (2021). *Soft CLIL and English language teaching: Understanding Japanese policy, practice and implications*. Routledge.

Jørgensen, J. N., Karrebæk, M. S., Madsen, L. M., & Møller, J. S. (2011). Polylanguaging in superdiversity. *Diversities*, 13(2), 23–37.

Leontjev, D., & DeBoer, M. (Eds.). (2020). *Assessment and learning in content and language integrated learning (CLIL) classrooms: Approaches and conceptualisations.* Springer Nature.

Marsh, D., & Frigols, M.-J. (2007). CLIL as a catalyst for change in language education. *Babylonia, 3*, 33–37.

Mehisto, P., Marsh, D., & Frigols, M. J. (2008). *Uncovering CLIL: Content and language integrated learning in bilingual and multilingual education.* Macmillan Education.

Meyer, O., Halbach, A., & Coyle, D. (2015). A pluriliteracies approach to teaching for learning. *ECML-Council of Europe.* Retrieved from https://pluriliteracies. ecml. at/Portals/54/publications/pluriliteracies-Putting-apluriliteracies-approach-into-practice. pdf.

Morton, T. (2010). Using a Genre-based approach to integrating content and language in CLIL. In C. Dalton-Puffer, T. Nikula, & U. Smit (Eds.), *Language use and language learning in CLIL classrooms* (pp. 81–104). John Benjamins.

Ortega, Y. (2019). "Teacher, ¿puedo hablar en español?" A reflection on plurilingualism and translanguaging practices in EFL. *Profile: Issues in Teachers' Professional Development, 21*(2), 155–170. https://doi.org/10.15446/profile.v21n2.74091

Pérez-Cañado, M. L. (2016). From the CLIL craze to the CLIL conundrum: Addressing the current CLIL controversy. *Bellaterra Journal of Teaching & Learning Language & Literature, 9*(1), 9–31. https://doi.org/10.5565/rev/jtl3.667

Pérez-Cañado, M. L. (2020). The what's, why's, who's, and how's of Andalusian plurilingual education. In M. Jiménez Raya, T. Lamb, & F. Vieira (Eds.), *Foreign language teaching in Europe* (pp. 39–64). Peter Lang.

Pérez Cañado, M. L. (2021). Inclusion and diversity in bilingual education: A European comparative study. *International Journal of Bilingual Education and Bilingualism,* 1–17. https://doi.org/10.1080/13670050.2021.2013770

Pérez Cañado, M. L., Rascón Moreno, D., & Cueva López, V. (2021). Identifying difficulties and best practices in catering to diversity in CLIL: Instrument design and validation. *International Journal of Bilingual Education and Bilingualism,* 1-9. https://doi.org/10.1080/13670050.2021.1988050

Pinner, R. (2019). *Authenticity and teacher-student motivational synergy: A narrative of language teaching.* Routledge.

Seikkula-Leino, J. (2007). CLIL learning: Achievement levels and affective factors. *Language and Education, 21*(4), 328–341. https://doi.org/10.2167/le635.0

Siepmann, P., Rumlich, D., Matz, F., & Römhild, R. (2021). Attention to diversity in German CLIL classrooms: Multi-perspective research on students' and teachers' perceptions. *International Journal of Bilingual Education and Bilingualism*, 1–17. https://doi.org/10.1080/13670050.2021.1981821

Tsuchiya, K. (2019). CLIL and language education in Japan. In T. Tsuchiya & M. D. Pérez Murillo (Eds.), *Content and language integrated learning in Spanish and Japanese contexts* (pp. 37–56). Cham: Palgrave Macmillan.

van Kampen, E., Meirink, J., Admiraal, W., & Berry, A. (2020). Do we all share the same goals for content and language integrated learning (CLIL)? Specialist and practitioner perceptions of 'ideal' CLIL pedagogies in the Netherlands. *International Journal of Bilingual Education and Bilingualism*, 23(8), 855–871. https://doi.org/10.1080/13670050.2017.1411332

Wei, R., & Feng, J. (2015). Implementing CLIL for young learners in an EFL context beyond Europe: Grassroots support and language policy in China. *English Today*, 31(1), 55–60. https://doi.org/10.1017/S0266078414000558

Part II. Assessing CLIL outcomes: Language and content learning and impact on the mother tongue

Chapter 3. Empirical studies on the effectiveness of CLIL for language learning

Abstract: This chapter is devoted to providing a general overview of the most relevant quantitative studies on language learning outcomes in CLIL. The primary interest of scholars was, without a doubt, to determine whether CLIL was effective in providing students with higher levels of proficiency in the target language. Since the main rationale behind CLIL provisions was improving language learning, appraising its effectiveness in attaining this main goal was obviously paramount and a priority in the CLIL research panorama. Early studies on language learning in CLIL were drawn upon systematic investigations conducted on immersion programmes in Canada, which detected immersion students acquired higher levels in their receptive skills (nearly native-like) than in their productive competences in the target language. In this vein, with the assertion that in the integrated learning "certain aspects of language competence are developed more than others", Dalton-Puffer (2008, p. 143) opened the floor in the European CLIL for the debate on the so-called "competencies favourably affected" and "competencies unaffected" by CLIL. This line of research has been very productive, and the body of studies framed in it seems to suggest that contrary to immersion programmes, CLIL contributes more positively to developing productive language skills than receptive ones. This oral language improvement is also being pursued in Asian traditional EFL contexts like Japan, where a "soft" version of CLIL is spreading around many institutions and education levels. A second phase in CLIL research was characterised by the publications of articles in which the validity of some of the studies conducted to date was questioned, casting doubt on the ascription to CLIL of the detected differences in language learning in favour of CLIL students. What is more, some of these investigations have accused CLIL of being elitist, attracting upper and upper middle classes and promoting segregation. A third stage in CLIL research captained by the Spanish researcher Pérez Cañado, endeavoured to obtain solid data on CLIL's impact on language learning and analysed elitism and attention to diversity in CLIL. These recent studies will be discussed in the last section of the chapter along with the examination of future lines of research on language proficiency in CLIL settings.Keywords: Language learning, oral and written competences, bilingual education, immersion, CLIL.

3.1. Language learning as the main rationale for CLIL

The overarching rationale behind the inception of CLIL, in 1994, was providing a framework for developing initiatives for bilingual education in an attempt to enhance multilingualism, improve language learning and raise deficient European standards (Pérez-Cañado & Ráez-Padilla, 2015). Although Europe is made up of a mosaic of languages, mutual understanding is crucial for its construction of Europe. Therefore, European institutions promoted the implementation of effective language learning approaches, since multilingualism was seen as a requirement to foster cohesion, a sense of identity, mobility and economic growth. Thus, drawing upon the success of immersion programmes in Canada, it was intended to transpose this model to the European context. For Marsh (2002, p. 11) CLIL was "a pragmatic European solution to a European need", i.e., a flexible concept or umbrella term to foster bilingual education. Hence, one of the main components of CLIL is that it is adaptable to particular language scenarios and needs across European countries.

In correlation with the main objective of CLIL, "the most prominent line of research taps into the effectiveness of CLIL for language learning" (Nieto Moreno de Diezmas, 2019, p. 73). In fact, San Isidro and Lasagabaster (2018, p. 2) highlight that research has most conspicuously addressed L2 development and underscore that "there is an outstanding imbalance between the number of studies focusing on English learning on the one hand, and those on content learning and L1 development on the other, to the detriment of the latter". Another reason behind this fact is that, as Merino and Lasagabaster (2018, p. 2) pinpoint, "many of the researchers involved in CLIL studies have been applied linguists", and as a result, their primary interest was focused on examining language learning outcomes. In the next section, the main studies looking into L2 development will be discussed, along with the main debates in the CLIL research arena.

3.2. The debate about the affected and unaffected language competences

One of the most prevalent interests of researches has been to determine the impact of CLIL on different language competences, areas, skills and subskills. In this regard, it is important to note that the initial investigations in the field were influenced by research results on the Canadian immersion. The main conclusions to be drawn from the extensive investigations carried out on these programmes were that immersion students "perform as well as native French-speaking students on tests of reading and listening comprehension in French" (Genesee, 1991, p. 186) but "they seldom achieve the same high levels of competence in speaking and writing as they achieve in comprehension" (Genesee, 1991, p. 186). In a nutshell, evidence showed that immersion contributed to improving receptive language competences to a greater extent than productive ones.

With these findings in mind, and after examining previous studies conducted to ascertain the impact of CLIL on language learning, Dalton-Puffer (2008) opened the floor for the discussion on favourably affected and unaffected language competences by CLIL methodology. As can be seen in Tab. 2, the first positively affected competences the author mentioned were receptive skills, outcome clearly in keeping with research findings on Canadian immersion programmes. Further benefits of CLIL were ascribed to vocabulary, morphology, creativity, fluency, and emotive and affective outcomes. Dalton-Puffer (2008) included the productive skill of "writing" among competences unaffected by CLIL, in line with the Canadian immersion dichotomy between receptive and productive skills, being the latter less positively developed. Syntax, informal language, pronunciation and pragmatics were also listed by Dalton-Puffer as aspects unaffected by the integrated learning.

Tab. 2: Affected and unaffected language competences

	Favourably affected	Unaffected or Indefinite
Language competences	Receptive skills Vocabulary Morphology Creativity, risk-taking, Fluency, quantity Emotive/affective outcomes	Syntax Writing Informal/non-technical language Pronunciation Pragmatics

Source: Own elaboration based on Dalton-Puffer (2008)

Ruiz de Zarobe (2011, pp. 145, 146), in turn, reviewed Dalton-Puffer's (2008) framework. In light of findings coming from updated studies, the list of positively affected competences increased. Productive skills, or at least some of their areas or subskills, were then included, since investigations have detected the contribution of CLIL to improving lexical richness in writing tasks (Jiménez Catalán et al., 2006) and in oral production (Hüttner & Rieder-Bünemann, 2007; Lasagabaster, 2008; Ruiz de Zarobe, 2008). As a result, Ruiz de Zarobe (2011) renewed the inventory of benefits of CLIL and established as positively affected competences the following ones: reading, listening, receptive vocabulary, speaking (fluency), writing (fluency and lexical and syntactic complexity), some morphological phenomena, and emotive and affective outcomes.

Nevertheless, the results of studies on Canadian immersion determined certain trends in CLIL research. In the first place, it was taken for granted that similarly to immersion, the areas CLIL would affect the most would be reading and listening. As a result, it was not considered urgent to look into these competences in depth, and as San Isidro and Lasagabaster (2018, p. 3) pinpointed "published research studies showing evidence of listening and reading development are few". At this point, it is important to note that immersion and CLIL differ not only in terms of sociolinguistic context, language command of teachers and language goals for students (Lasagabaster & Sierra, 2009), but there are also dissimilarities between these approaches regarding research goals and design (see Chapter 1). Thus, in immersion, the language goal for students is to attain native-like proficiency, and consequently, the investigations have compared L2 proficiency of immersion students with native speakers. The main objective of CLIL, in view of the limited efficiency of traditional classes of foreign languages art, is to implement alternative and enriched language learning methodologies. Accordingly, to check if CLIL provides more effective learning than the subject of foreign language, the researchers have compared language achievement of CLIL learners to non-CLIL students in regular programmes, and not to native speakers, unlike the investigations on immersion did. Hence, as Pérez-Cañado (2012, p. 318) highlights, immersion research findings "cannot be simply transferred or transposed to the European scenario". Furthermore, it seems that, contrary to research results on immersion, in the long term "it was productive, as opposed to receptive, skills which were more positively affected by CLIL" (Pérez-Cañado, 2018, p. 54).

In addition to the debate focused on productive versus receptive skills, another important issue in CLIL research has been to determine its impact on oral competences. The communicative approach and the more naturalistic scenario CLIL provides were expected to contribute to enhancing oral competences. In fact, the improvement of oral competences was one of the desired and purported benefits of CLIL already mentioned in Eurydice Report (2006). However, initial findings related to productive and receptive oral skills have been inconsistent, probably due to shortage of studies in this area, along with differences in the methodology of the studies, age of students, and type of school (public/private) among other factors. Since the investigation on oral competences emerges as one of the most contentious aspects in CLIL research, the main studies tapping into this aspect will be addressed in the next section.

3.3. CLIL and development of oral skills

3.3.1. The case of listening comprehension

Listening and oral production are two competences expected to record significant improvement by the effect of delivering subjects in the target language, due to the consequent increased students-teacher and student-student interaction opportunities. However, in the case of listening, "no clear conclusions can be drawn" (Ruiz de Zarobe, 2015, p. 56). Maybe one of the reasons behind this assertion is the dearth of studies looking into this skill. Hence, in words of Prieto-Arranz et al. (2015, p. 216), "the lack of research is perhaps especially all the more evident in the field of listening comprehension".

If we analyse in depth the existent studies, two overarching trends may be identified. In the first place, oral comprehension seems to benefit from CLIL to a lesser extent than other language skills and needs a longer time span to be significantly affected. Secondly, listening competences, as the rest of language competences, result positively benefitted in the long term.

Thus, the studies carried out by Stotz and Meuter (2003), Lasagabaster (2008), Navés (2011), Pladevall-Ballester and Vallbona (2016) Pérez-Vidal and Roquet (2015), Nieto Moreno de Diezmas (2016), and Pérez-Cañado and Lancaster (2017) illustrate the aforementioned first conclusion: listening competence specifically needs more time to be positively affected by CLIL.

In Zurich (Switzerland) Stotz and Meuter (2003) observed limited advances in the listening of primary school learners who had received only 90–100 minutes a week of content subjects in English. In the Basque Country (Spain), Lasagabaster (2008) looked into CLIL programmes in secondary school and compared CLIL students to 1-year-older non-CLIL learners. The CLIL group scored higher in oral and written production, but not in listening. Likewise, in Catalonia, Navés (2011) detected that CLIL students showed similar competence to non-CLIL learners 2 or 3 years older in all proficiency tests: cloze, dictation and grammar, except for the listening test. Pladevall-Ballester and Vallbona (2016) compared the contribution to English learning in three different scenarios: (a) learning arts and crafts in English, (b) learning science in English, and (c) receiving the equivalent exposure time as in the two aforementioned scenarios through the English subject as a foreign language (EFL). There were no significant differences in listening comprehension between non-CLIL students exposed to English through the English language subject and the CLIL group of science, but interestingly enough, the non-CLIL learners significantly outperformed the CLIL group of arts and crafts. The authors concluded that "EFL-only exposure is more effective in the development of young learners' listening skills in the short-term" (Pladevall-Ballester & Vallbona, 2016), and considered more time is needed to observe the purported positive effects of CLIL.

In the same vein Pérez-Vidal and Roquet (2015) observed that in a 2-year span, CLIL students significantly outstripped their non-CLIL peers in writing and reading but not in listening. The authors explained those results because of the limited exposure to English offered by only one CLIL content subject and suggested more exposure to CLIL would be needed to observe improvements. In turn, Nieto Moreno de Diezmas (2016) detected CLIL learners in primary education of a monolingual Spanish autonomous community located in central Spain significantly outperformed their non-CLIL peers in speaking, and obtained higher scores in reading and writing, whereas in listening, they recorded lower scores. As for the investigation conducted by Pérez Cañado and Lancaster (2017) in Andalusia, more optimistic results were found for listening. However, although significant gains in favour of the CLIL group were observed in grade 4 of compulsory secondary education (CSE), these differences between CLIL and non-CLIL students in listening did not pervade once the CLIL group entered the regular post-compulsory programme.

The second trend aforementioned is that listening skills are positively affected with extensive exposure or in the long run, namely in secondary school. This conclusion can be illustrated by the studies carried by Nieto Moreno de Diezmas (2018), Pérez-Cañado (2018), and San Isidro and Lasagabaster (2018). Nieto Moreno de Diezmas (2018) looked into listening skills development in primary and secondary education. The study unveiled that in primary school significant differences in favour of the CLIL group were found only in two subskills: global comprehension and identification of details. In secondary education, CLIL students significant outperformed in all the six subskills considered in the study: global comprehension, identification of details, understanding of the situation of communication, oral receptive vocabulary, understanding of paralinguistic elements, and identification of space-time relations. These findings were ascribed to the fact that CLIL effectiveness is deployed in the long term. Sustained exposure to CLIL was considered to be fundamental along with the cognitive development of secondary school students that enabled them to take full advantage of the approach.

This conclusion is in keeping with Pérez-Cañado's (2018) study, since she did not find significantly higher levels in the listening of CLIL students (except for the ones enrolled in private schools) at the end of primary education, whereas in secondary school, the CLIL branch outperformed their non-CLIL peers in all skills, and with wider differences, thereby concluding that "the longer the students have been benefitting from bilingual education, the greater the differences with their non-bilingual counterparts" (Pérez-Cañado, 2018, p. 61). In the same vein, San Isidro and Lasagabaster (2018), also identified a positive effect of CLIL on listening skills in secondary schoolers enrolled in a CLIL programme implemented in Galicia (Spain).

In contrast, it is worth mentioning a longitudinal study by Merino and Lasagabaster (2018) that concluded that CLIL students entered secondary school with a significantly higher listening competence, but, over a year the CLIL group did not progress more than the non-CLIL group did. These contradictory findings come to season what was described by Pérez-Cañado and Lancaster (2017, p. 2) as a "vibrant research scene".

3.3.2. Oral production as the most evident benefit

Although in Canadian immersion more benefits were detected for receptive than productive language skills, very soon studies on CLIL started to deviate from this dichotomy. In fact, Dalton Puffer (2011, p. 187) stated "the area where a difference between CLIL students and mainstream learners is most noticeable is their spontaneous oral production". Most of the studies conducted to ascertain the contribution of CLIL to the development of oral production have been set in secondary education. Despite the scarcity of investigations looking into speaking outcomes in primary education, it is worth mentioning two studies (Nieto Moreno de Diezmas, 2016; Pérez-Cañado, 2018) working with significant samples and conducted in monolingual autonomous communities of Spain.

The first one (Nieto Moreno de Diezmas, 2016) was carried out in five provinces of central Spain. No significant differences between CLIL and non-CLIL learners in grade 4 of primary education were observed in the overall evaluation of reading, writing and listening, except for some of the subskills considered: preparing an outline before writing (writing), understanding space-time relations (reading), global comprehension and identification of details (listening). However, CLIL 4 graders significantly outperformed their non-CLIL peers in overall oral production and in every single subskill examined: vocabulary, fluency, rhythm, pronunciation and intonation, preparation of the interaction, answering questions, active listening, and respect for the rules of communicative exchange. In contrast to listening, results indicated that oral production was the most rapidly benefitted competence from CLIL.

Pérez-Cañado (2018), in turn, assessed primary education students 2 years older (grade 6) from twelve Spanish provinces enrolled in fifty-three schools. The researcher found the greater benefits of CLIL were recorded in oral production, with significant gains in all subskills sampled (pronunciation, grammar, vocabulary, fluency, and content), which falls in line with the aforementioned study (Nieto Moreno de Diezmas, 2016).

Regarding secondary education, Hüttner and Rieder-Bünemann (2007) conducted in Austria a ground-breaking study aimed at assessing CLIL and non-CLIL students' oral production. Participants were enrolled in forty-four secondary schools, and results indicated the CLIL group showed a better command in micro- and macro-level narrative aspects. The authors ascribed these findings to the CLIL approach, although they brought to the fore the fact that CLIL students seemed to be more strongly motivated. In Spain, the scientific literature in this field has been more prolific compared to other European countries. In this regard, three studies set in secondary education were located in the Basque Country and conducted by: Ruiz de Zarobe (2008), Lasagabaster (2008) and Villarreal Olaizola and García Mayo (2009).

Ruiz de Zarobe (2008) compared CLIL with no-CLIL students who were one year older with a similar number of hours of exposure to English: the first group through CLIL and the second group, exclusively through the subject of English (EFL). The CLIL group, even if they were younger, outperformed the EFL group in pronunciation, vocabulary, grammar, fluency and content. The main conclusion drawn from the study was that oral production competence benefitted more from L2 exposure through CLIL than through an EFL approach. Similarly, Lasagabaster (2008) observed that CLIL students outstripped non-CLIL learners one grade ahead in oral production. In the same vein, Villarreal Olaizola and García Mayo (2009) detected CLIL contributed to improving accuracy in oral productions, particularly morpheme omission and error frequency.

In contrast, in the Balearic Islands, Rallo Fabra and Jacob (2015) found, though, no differences in the fluency of oral productions of CLIL and non-CLIL students over the course of two years. However, the study carried out by Pérez-Cañado and Lancaster (2017) looking into the Andalusian CLIL programme did observe CLIL significantly impacted overall speaking competence, particularly in grammar, vocabulary, task fulfilment and fluency, which was the subskill with higher differences in the mean score in favour of the CLIL group. The marked advantage of CLIL students in this skill was associated with the following factors: the extensive practice provided, fundamental in a skill which "requires the most training" (Pérez-Cañado & Lancaster, 2017), the implementation of the communicative approach, and the fact that students were being prepared during the CLIL lessons to attain the A2 certificate of the Common European Framework of Reference (CEFR). Additionally, the authors uncovered that the gains in oral production were more solid than the improvement in oral reception since the benefits in speaking pervaded 6 months later. These findings tally with the study developed by Pérez Cañado (2018) who found CLIL students were significantly ahead in oral production and six months later, differences "not only pervade, but become even stronger" (Pérez Cañado, 2018, p. 62).

One of the subskills of oral production which deserves special attention is the pronunciation, an area in which studies are inconclusive. Gallardo del Puerto et al. (2009) concluded that CLIL did not contribute to improving the degree of foreign accent, possibly because CLIL teachers were not natives but foreign speakers of the L2. However, CLIL students' accent was significantly more intelligible and less irritating. Rallo Fabra and Jacob's (2015) study found even less optimistic results, since no differences were found between CLIL and non-CLIL students in pronunciation, and no progress was recorded after two years of CLIL. Interestingly, Pérez-Cañado and Lancaster (2017) detected CLIL students significantly outperformed non-CLIL learners in all the areas of spoken production except for pronunciation. In this case, contrary to the study by Gallardo del Puerto et al. (2009), the English teacher of both groups was native, and maybe that fact approached pronunciation of CLIL and non-CLIL students. With a considerably greater sample, Pérez-Cañado (2018) in a subsequent study did identify significant differences between CLIL and non-CLIL groups in all subskills of oral production, including pronunciation both in secondary and primary school. In conclusion, more studies are required to better understand the development of this skill in CLIL environments.

3.4. Critical views on the contribution of CLIL to language learning

Although, in general terms, most of the studies carried out in the field ascribe positive effects to CLIL, some critical views harboured by authors such as Bruton (2011, 2013, 2015, 2019), and Paran (2013) have questioned the validity of the investigations and the effectiveness of the approach.

Pérez-Cañado (2016, 2017) has encompassed these dismissive narratives into a general cycle experienced by the innovations in language learning over history, already identified and coined by Swan (1985) as a "pendulum effect". The pendulum effect observed in CLIL is characterised by a very hopeful initial reception, which produced, in the words of Paran (2013, p. 334), a "celebratory rhetoric", followed by swinging of the pendulum to the opposite side. The result of this movement is "a dismal, pessimistic outlook on the feasibility of CLIL implementation", which "questions the validity of the research conducted" and "even warns of the dangers of its application (Pérez Cañado, 2017, p. 2). Furthermore, these negative narratives are not restricted to the scientific literature but have also permeated the mass media and have "become viral among families and schools" (Nieto Moreno de Diezmas & Hill, 2019, p. 179).

One of the main accusations against CLIL was that it is selective, or at least self-selective (Bruton, 2011), and as a result, CLIL detractors brought to the fore that CLIL students possibly were already more proficient in English and more motivated before entering the programme, and that would be the reason why they performed better. Against this backdrop, Pérez Cañado (2017) observed some shortcomings in previous studies and suggested specific ways to supersede those possible lacunae. For example, the author recommended that intervening variables should be controlled, and CLIL and non-CLIL students matched in terms of verbal intelligence, motivation, sociocultural level, level of English, and extramural exposure. Differences between CLIL and non-CLIL learners should be scrutinised by means of ANOVA and t-test, and factor and discriminant analyses should be carried out to ascertain whether those differences can be genuinely ascribed to CLIL. A combination of quantitative and qualitative research methods was also advised by Pérez-Cañado (2017), along with the development of longitudinal studies.

3.5. Updated empirical studies on language outcomes and future paths ahead

From the outset, the overriding intention of researchers was to determine whether language gains could be attributed to CLIL methodology and not uniquely to the increased exposure to the L2 that the approach entails. With this idea in mind, studies such as the ones carried out by Lasagabaster (2008), Ruiz de Zarobe (2008) and Navés (2011) compared CLIL learners with non-CLIL counterparts one, two or three courses ahead. This way, researchers could guarantee both groups had received a similar number of hours in the L2: non-CLIL students by means of the subject of foreign language, and the CLIL group, both through the subject of foreign language and the content subjects imparted in the L2. Most of this first handful of studies were cross-sectional.

After the critiques expounded in the previous section, a second wave of studies such as Pérez Cañado and Lancaster's (2017), Merino and Lasagabaster's (2018), Pérez-Cañado's (2018), and San Isidro and Lasagabaster's (2018), among others, have tried to overcome the shortcomings detected in the design of the research conducted to date. Interestingly enough, most of the findings of these longitudinal studies using meticulous statistical analyses backed up results and trends already found in previous cross-sectional investigations.

In this vein, it is important to highlight the validity and conclusive character of the findings of the study conducted by Pérez-Cañado (2018). The design of this investigation was one of the most robust to date: (i) the sample was considerable (1,033 CLIL and 991 non-CLIL learners from 53 public, private, and charter schools of 12 Spanish provinces); (ii) the homogeneity between the groups was guarantee by means of a pre-test on English level, verbal intelligence and motivation; (iii) post- and a delayed post-test were used; (iv) intergroup and intragroup evolution was studied, and (v) discriminant analyses were carried out to determine the impact of intervening variables. Results of this study showed significant differences in overall proficiency in the L2 in favour of the CLIL group. These differences were already perceptible in primary education and more marked in secondary school. The discriminant analyses indicated that CLIL was truly responsible for those differences, since they were better explained by the bilingual programme than by verbal intelligence, extramural exposure to English, motivation, type of school or socioeconomic status. Drawing upon this study, the benefits of CLIL for L2 development are unquestionable. In addition, evidence showed differences in favour of CLIL students were not due to socioeconomic status, which counters the accusation of elitism in these programmes.

More evidence refuting elitism in CLIL can be found in the study conducted by Nieto Moreno de Diezmas (2019). Primary schoolers from five provinces in Spain were distributed, according to their competences in L2, in six achievement bands or proficiency levels (very low, low, low-intermediate, intermediate, upper-intermediate, and high). Findings indicated that precisely CLIL contributed to a greater extent than regular programmes to reducing the percentage of students with the lowest levels of proficiency. In contrast, traditional classes of L2 were more detrimental for the students at risk and more beneficial for the most gifted students. As a result, CLIL made a difference by providing more opportunities for all, and showing its potential to fight against school failure and promote equity in education.

So, what is next on the CLIL research agenda? In the first place, after almost 20 years of the inception of CLIL, the improvement of the quality of the programmes continues to be an overriding objective for all stakeholders. To contribute to developing CLIL, more research is needed, since as it has been already pinpointed by the scientific literature (Fernández Fontecha, 2009; Nieto Moreno de Diezmas & Hill, 2019; Pérez-Cañado, 2018, 2020) the flexibility of the approach produces a variety of implementations, and every context needs to be analysed in order to detect its particular improvement areas (see Chapter 2). The number and type of CLIL subjects, teaching methodologies, translanguaging and role of languages in the classroom vary from programme to programme and even from school to school and need to be considered and studied by means of quantitative and qualitative research methods. Another area which deserves further scrutiny is the way the academic discourse functions (Dalton-Puffer, 2013) are scaffolded in the classroom against the backdrop of the specific disciplinary literacy of every subject. The conjugation between the development of cognitive academic language proficiency (CALP), basic interpersonal communication skills (CALP), and classroom language needs to be addressed in terms of both teacher practice and training.

In general terms, more information about the development of top-down and bottom-up processes is required to better understand the functioning of these programmes. Particularly, it would be enlightening to study how theoretical frameworks and research findings are incorporated in the design of educational policies, and how these policies are understood and implemented at school and classroom levels across different programmes, contexts and countries.

Bibliography

Bruton, A. (2011). Is CLIL so beneficial, or just selective? Re-evaluating some of the research. *System, 39*(4), 523–532. https://doi.org/10.1016/j.system.2011.08.002

Bruton, A. (2013).) CLIL: Some of the reasons why... and why not. *System, 41,* 587–597.

Bruton, A. (2015). CLIL: Detail matters in the whole picture. More than a reply to J. Hüttner and U. Smit (2014). *System, 53,* 119–128. https://doi.org/10.1016/j.system.2015.07.005

Bruton, A. (2019). Questions about CLIL which are unfortunately still not outdated: A reply to Pérez-Cañado. *Applied Linguistics Review, 10*(4), 591–602. https://doi.org/10.1515/applirev-2017-0059

Dalton-Puffer, C. (2008). Outcomes and processes in CLIL: Current research from Europe. In W. Delanoy & L. Volkman (Eds.), *Future perspectives for English language teaching* (pp. 139–158). Carl Winter.

Dalton-Puffer, C. (2013). A construct of cognitive discourse functions for conceptualising content-language integration in CLIL and multilingual education. *European Journal of Applied Linguistics, 1*(2). https://doi.org/10.1515/eujal-2013-0011

Eurydice Report. (2006). *Content and language integrated learning (CLIL) at school in Europe.* Brussels Eurydice.

Fernández Fontecha, A. (2009). Spanish CLIL: Research and official actions. In Y. Ruiz de Zarobe & M. Jiménez Catalán (Eds.), *Content and language integrated learning. Evidence from research in Europe* (pp. 3–21). Multilingual Matters.

Gallardo del Puerto, F., García Lecumberri, M., & Gómez Lacabex, E. (2009). Testing the effectiveness of content and language integrated learning in foreign language contexts: Assessment of English pronunciation. In Y. Ruiz de Zarobe & R. M. Jiménez Catalán (Eds.), *Content and language integrated learning: Evidence from research in Europe* (pp. 215–234). Multilingual Matters.

Genesee, F. (1991). Second language learning in schools settings: Lessons from immersion. In A. Reynolds (Ed.), *Bilingualism, multiculturalism, and second language learning* (pp. 183–201). Lawrence Erlbaum.

Hüttner, J., & Rieder-Bünemann, A. (2007). The effect of CLIL instruction on children's narrative competence. *VIEWS Vienna English Working Papers, 16*(3), 20–27.

Jiménez Catalán, R. M., Ruiz de Zarobe, Y., & Cenoz, J. (2006). Vocabulary profiles of English Foreign Language learners in English as a subject and as a vehicular language. *Views, 15*(3), 23–27.

Johnson, R. K., & Swain, M. (1997). *Immersion education: International perspectives.* Cambridge university Press.

Lambert, W. E., & Tucker, G. R. (1972). *Bilingual education of children. The St. Lambert experiment.* Newbury House.

Lasagabaster, D. (2008). Foreign language competence in content and language integrated learning. *Open Applied Linguistics Journal, 1*, 31–42. https://doi.org/10.2174/1874913500801010030

Lasagabaster, D., & Sierra, J. M. (2009). Immersion and CLIL in English: More differences than similarities. *ELT Journal, 63*(4), 67–375. https://doi:10.1093/elt/ccp082

Marsh, D. (2002). *CLIL/EMILE- The European dimension. Actions, trends and foresight potential.* Unicom, Continuing Education Centre.

Mehisto, P., Marsh, D., & Frigols, M. J. (2008). *Uncovering CLIL, content and language integrated learning in bilingual and multilingual education.* Macmillan.

Merino, J. A., & Lasagabaster, D. (2018). CLIL as a way to multilingualism. *International Journal of Bilingual Education and Bilingualism, 21*, 79–92 https://doi.org/10.1080/13670050.2015.1128386

Navés, T. (2011). How promising are the results of integrating content and language for EFL writing and overall EFL proficiency? In Y. Ruiz de Zarobe, J. M. Sierra & F. Gallardo del Puerto (Eds.), *Content and foreign language integrated learning: Contributions to multilingualism in European contexts* (pp. 103–128). Peter Lang.

Nieto Moreno de Diezmas, E. (2016). The impact of CLIL on the acquisition of language competences and skills in L2 in primary education. *International Journal of English Studies, 16*(2), 81–102. https://doi.org/10.6018/ijes/2016/2/239611

Nieto Moreno de Diezmas, E. (2018). The acquisition of L2 listening Comprehension skills in primary and secondary education settings: A comparison between CLIL and non-CLIL student performance. *RLA. Revista de Lingüística*

Teórica y Aplicada, 56(2), 13–34. http://dx.doi.org/10.4067/S0718-488320 18000200013

Nieto Moreno de Diezmas, E. (2019). The effect of CLIL on the distribution of primary students in language proficiency levels: A case study in Castilla-La Mancha. In A. Jiménez-Muñoz & A. C. Lahuerta Martínez (Eds.), *Empirical studies in multilingualism. Analysing contexts and outcomes* (pp. 73–101). Peter Lang. https://doi.org/10.3726/b15231

Nieto Moreno de Diezmas, E., & y Hill, T. M. (2019). Social science learning and gender-based differences in CLIL. A preliminary study. *Estudios de lingüística inglesa aplicada (ELIA), 19*, 177–204. http://dx.doi.org/10.12795/elia.2019. i19.08

Paran, A. (2013). Content and language integrated learning: Panacea or policy borrowing myth? *Applied Linguistics Review, 4*(2), 317–342. https://doi. org/ 10.1515/applirev-2013-0014

Pérez-Cañado, M. L. (2012). CLIL research in Europe: Past, present and future. *International Journal of Bilingual Education and Bilingualism, 15*(3), 315–341. https://doi:10.1080/13670050.2011.630064

Pérez-Cañado, M. L. (2016). From the CLIL craze to the CLIL conundrum: Addressing the current CLIL controversy. *Bellaterra Journal of Teaching & Learning Language & Literature, 9*(1), 9–31. https://doi.org/10.5565/rev/jtl3.667

Pérez Cañado, M. L. (2017). Stopping the "pendulum effect" in CLIL research: Finding the balance between Pollyanna and Scrooge. *Applied Linguistics Review, 8*(1), 79–99. https://doi.org/10.1515/applirev-2016-2001

Pérez Cañado, M. L. (2018). CLIL and educational level: A longitudinal study on the impact of CLIL on language outcomes. *Porta Linguarum, 29*, 51–70. https://doi.org/10.30827/digibug.54022

Pérez Cañado, M. L. (2020). What's hot and what's not on the current CLIL research agenda: Weeding out the non-issues from the real issues. A response to Bruton (2019). *Applied Linguistics Review.* https://doi.org/10.1515/applirev-2020-0033

Pérez-Cañado, M. L., & Ráez-Padilla, J. (2015). Introduction and overview. In D. Marsh, M. L. Pérez Cañado, & J. Ráez Padilla (Eds.), *CLIL in action: Voices from the classroom* (pp. 1–12). Cambridge Scholars Publishing.

Pérez-Cañado, M. L., & Lancaster, N. (2017). The effects of CLIL on oral comprehension and production: A longitudinal case study. *Language, Culture, and Curriculum, 30*(3), 300–316. https://doi.org/10.1080/07908318.2017.1338717

Pérez-Vidal, C., & Roquet, H. (2015). CLIL in context: Profiling language abilities. In M. Juan-Garau & J. Salazar Noguera (Eds.), *Content-based language learning in multilingual educational environments* (pp. 237–255). Springer. https://doi.org/10.1007/978-3-319-11496-5_14

Pladevall-Ballester, E., & Vallbona, A. (2016). CLIL in minimal input contexts: A longitudinal study of primary school learners' receptive skills. *System, 58,* 37–48. https://doi.org/10.1016/j.system.2016.02.009

Prieto-Arranz, J. I., Rallo Fabra, L., Calafat-Ripoll, C., & Catrain González, M. (2015). Testing progress on receptive skills in CLIL and non-CLIL contexts. In M. Juan-Garau & J. Salazar Noguera (Eds.), *Content-based language learning in multilingual educational environments* (pp. 123–137). Springer.

Rallo Fabra, L., & Jacob, K. (2015). Does CLIL enhance oral skills? Fluency and pronunciation errors by Spanish-Catalan learners of English. In M. Juan-Garau & J. Salazar Noguera (Eds.), *Content-based language learning in multilingual educational environments* (pp. 163–177). Springer. https://doi.org/10.1007/978-3-319-11496-5_10

Ruiz de Zarobe, Y. (2008). CLIL and foreign language learning: A longitudinal study in the Basque country. *International CLIL Research Journal, 1*(1), 60–73.

Ruiz de Zarobe, Y. (2011). Which language competencies benefit from CLIL? An insight into applied linguistics research. In Y. Ruiz de Zarobe, J. M. Sierra & F. Gallardo del Puerto (Eds.), *Content and foreign language integrated learning: Contributions to multilingualism in European contexts* (pp. 129–153). Peter Lang.

Ruiz de Zarobe, Y. (2015). The effects of implementing CLIL in education. In M. Juan-Garau & J. Salazar Noguera (Eds.), *Content-based language learning in multilingual educational environments* (pp. 51–67). Springer.

San Isidro, X., & Lasagabaster, D. (2018). The impact of CLIL on pluriliteracy development and content learning in a rural multilingual setting: A longitudinal study. *Language Teaching Research.* http://doi.org/10.1177/1362168817754103

Stotz, D., & Meuter, T. (2003). Embedded English: Integrating content and language learning in a Swiss primary school project. *Le Bulletin Suisse de Linguistique Appliquée, 77,* 83–101.

Swan, M. (1985). A critical look at the communicative approach (2). *ELT Journal, 39*(2), 76–87. http://dx.doi.org/10.1093/elt/39.2.76

Chapter 4. Content acquisition in CLIL settings: From pedagogical guidelines to empirical outcomes

Abstract: This chapter is devoted to exploring one of the overriding components of the binominal expressed in the acronym "CLIL" (content and language integrated learning): the content. This focus inevitably leads us to address one of the cornerstones of CLIL, which is the concept of integration itself. In this regard, it is paramount to highlight that preservation of the contents is essential to guarantee the sustainability of the approach. The curriculum cannot be sacrificed to additional or second language learning, even if multilingualism is a primary educational objective. The different elements of the curriculum (competences, objectives and content) are fundamental components to equip future citizens with the necessary knowledge, skills and values to actively perform in their adult life and for lifelong learning. Against this backdrop, it stands to reason that adequate assimilation of the curriculum has emerged as an overarching concern for all stakeholders involved: administration, schools, teachers and families. Consequently, and even if this area has produced fewer studies in comparison with language learning, diverse investigations have been undertaken to ascertain whether content learning is at risk in CLIL settings. The chapter is organised as follows. In the first section, the role of contents in CLIL will be analysed, considering the different versions of CLIL: language-oriented or soft CLIL and content-oriented or hard CLIL. The chapter goes on inscribing CLIL within the integrated curriculum approach and reflecting on the nature of integration in CLIL settings, followed by the enunciation of the main pedagogical frameworks to successfully integrate language and content. Finally, the most conspicuous issues pertaining to content, such as concept simplification or unsatisfactory acquisition, will be examined under the lens of empirical studies conducted in the field. The chapter ends with a reflection on the foresight of future research lines.

Keywords: Content learning, bilingual education, integrated learning, CLIL methodology

4.1. The role of contents in CLIL

The conceptualisation of the role of contents in CLIL pertains to the controversial definition of the approach, as seen in Chapters 1 and 2. As CLIL was conceived as "an umbrella label" (Dalton-Puffer & Smit, 2007, p. 8), it is an arduous task to locate CLIL in the continuum established by Met (1998), which ranges from content-driven to language-driven instruction (Fig. 7). In content-driven instruction, language learning is not the main rationale behind the implementation of the programme. This is the case of English-Medium Instruction (EMI) in university settings, since the main objective which underpins the adoption of this approach is generally linked to competing in the global market and improving the universities' international reputation and their position in global rankings, thereby "attracting international students and staff" (Nieto Moreno de Diezmas & Fernández Barrera, 2021, p. 40). In these contexts, English learning is incidental, and language is not explicitly taught, given that, according to the stakeholders, "content is king" (Airey, 2020, p. 343), the transmission of academic knowledge is to be preserved, and lecturers are not English specialist and do not consider teaching English is within their remit (Airey, 2012).

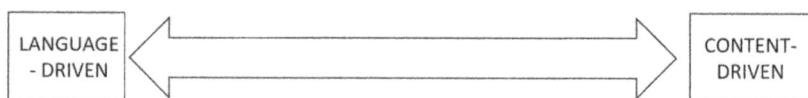

| LANGUAGE - DRIVEN | ⟸⟹ | CONTENT- DRIVEN |

Fig. 7: Continuum from language to content-driven. Source: based on Met (1998)

In the opposite end, in language-driven instruction, the contents are mere scenarios to better accomplish language learning, which is the priority. This approach is becoming increasingly popular in English Language Teaching (ELT) course books, which usually include a final section in each unit with curricular contents related to literature, geography, history, science, etc. These contents are addressed as cross-curricular themes in the English as Foreign Language (EFL) subject, where the overriding goal is learning English. This version of CLIL is called "soft CLIL" or type B CLIL (Massler et al., 2014). The reasons behind including cross-curricular contents in the subject of English language are manyfold. For example, this soft CLIL can be a complement in bilingual education settings, where school subjects, such as science or art, are taught through a second language, thus coexisting with "hard CLIL" programmes. This way, the insertion in the English course book of contents coming from these disciplines is used to reinforce concepts, vocabulary, or grammar structures related to them.

In other contexts, this language-led CLIL is being implemented as a way to put into practice more naturalistic teaching methodologies (Ikeda et al. 2021), since language is learnt while using it to learn about the world that surrounds the students (Marsh & Langé, 2000), which is a similar environment to the acquisition of L1. Additionally, this approach allows for shifting from the focus on the form of traditional classes of English language to a focus on meaning, thereby providing more motivating, interesting and less stressful learning environments. This "soft CLIL" characterised by including content-based themes in the classes of the language subject is gaining momentum in recent years with its rapid dissemination in Asian contexts, particularly, in Japan (cf. Chapter 1).

The "original" CLIL, however, is connected to "hard CLIL", or type A CLIL (Massler et al., 2014) and refers to the use of an additional language other than the mother tongue as the medium of instruction for school subjects. In fact, the inception of the acronym was linked to the idea of coining a European label to encompass and promote initiatives in keeping with immersion and bilingual education programmes which were being successfully implemented in Canada and North America. In this vein, CLIL was seen as a way to provide increased exposure to the target language within the school hours. In accordance with this conceptualisation, CLIL is defined as an: "educational approach where subjects such as geography or biology are taught through the medium of a foreign language" (Dalton-Puffer et al., 2010, p. 1). The most popular definition of CLIL established by Mehisto et al. is along similar lines; CLIL is depicted as "a dual-focused educational approach in which an additional language is used for the learning and teaching of both content and language" (2008, p. 9). It is precisely in this context, where the complexities of the "dual focus" arise.

In this "hard CLIL" or type A CLIL, the contents are not scenarios for language learning, but they acquire genuine curricular dimension, as essential constituents of the academic training of future citizens. Against this backdrop, the dual focus must be interpreted, more than as a balance between learning language and learning contents, as the need to guarantee both the acquisition of contents and the instructional language. Otherwise, all the educational innovation and institutional effort involved in the implementation of CLIL would be pointless.

As described in Chapter 1 CLIL was promoted by the European Union as a way to enhance multilingualism and intercultural competences of European citizens. Proficiency in various languages, including heritage and international languages, was essential for building a cohesive Europe with mutual understanding among its peoples. To achieve this goal, CLIL was embraced with the hope of improving unsatisfactory standards derived from traditional approaches based on grammar, accuracy, and form, which were unable to enhance communication, confidence, and fluency. However, despite it being a major objective for the European institutions, it is of utmost importance to preserve the quality of the educational systems and design an approach that does not jeopardise the integral development of the individuals.

It is, thus, fundamental to bear in mind that CLIL is, above all, "an educational approach" (Dalton-Puffer et al., 2010, p. 1; Mehisto et al., 2008, p. 9) developed within the curricular system of formal education. The prescriptive framework established by the corresponding educational administrations is made up of curricular elements (key competences, objectives, contents, and assessment criteria) that define educational priorities and determine the essential knowledge, skills, and attitudes for the future citizens to achieve in their personal, social, academic, and work life. As a result, the curriculum acts as a reference for the teaching-learning process for all schools regardless of whether they are implementing CLIL programmes or not. Therefore, if bilingual programmes cannot safeguard adequate acquisition of contents, along with the aforementioned curricular elements, the whole programme could be at risk, due to unsatisfactory content acquisition.

4.2. The integrated learning in formal education

Language and content are not separate entities. Even in mainstream education in which the majority language is used for the instruction, language competence determines the access to knowledge, and it is, therefore, an issue to address in multilingual and multicultural schools. However, the historical parcellation of knowledge into disciplinary areas does not contribute to open interdisciplinary ways of interrelations among contents from different areas and between language and contents. In a nutshell, the organisation of the curriculum itself "perpetuates the separation of language and content" (Stryker & Leaver, 1997, p. 7).

This segregation of realities that, nevertheless, goes hand in hand is to be avoided in educational proposals connected to the idea of the integrated curriculum. The integrated curriculum pursuits innovative practice aimed at overcoming the traditional disciplinary canon. In this approach, students engage in projects, tasks, and research, related to real-life problems from an interdisciplinary perspective (Fogarty, 1991; Humphreys et al., 1981). This way, learners are provided with more holistic outlooks of knowledge, and language is learnt in an integrated way, while used to access, process and express knowledge in a social context.

In keeping with this integrated view of the curriculum, the Council of the European Union has been promoting a theoretical and practical framework by means of its recommendations on key competences for lifelong learning (European Council, 2006, 2019). Key competences are selected for being considered "essential to citizens for personal fulfilment, a healthy and sustainable lifestyle, employability, active citizenship and social inclusion" (European Council, 2019, p. 4). The eight key competences established by the European Council are listed in Fig. 8.

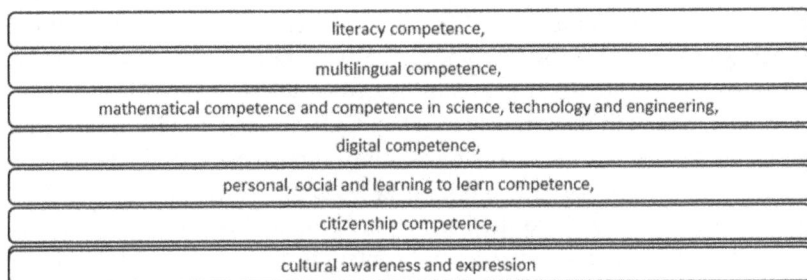

literacy competence,
multilingual competence,
mathematical competence and competence in science, technology and engineering,
digital competence,
personal, social and learning to learn competence,
citizenship competence,
cultural awareness and expression

Fig. 8: Key competences. Source: Based on European Council (2019)

To be competent, according to this framework, is to be able to act and solve problems in real-life situations by applying knowledge, skills and attitudes appropriate to the context. These competences are action-oriented, multifunctional and transferable to different contexts, and even more interestingly, they are cross-curricular, which means that all subjects should contribute to acquiring them. For example, science teachers should promote the development not only of the third competence "mathematical competence and competence in science, technology and engineering", but the integrated acquisition of all the key competences, including literacy and multilingual competence.

This general trend in education provides a comprehensive framework to apply and adapt to CLIL settings. CLIL seems, in fact, a scenario conducive to the implementation of a competence-based approach. According to Clegg (2014, p. 83) CLIL pedagogy "raises some competences … to the surface of classroom discourse" and "is cross-curricular in nature", since "it teaches some cross-cutting competences explicitly" (Clegg, 2014, p. 84). That is the case of learning to learn competence, which seems to be a key competence explicitly addressed in CLIL classrooms to help students face the double cognitive effort they make when learning new contents through and second language. As a result, CLIL students seem to have more developed metacognitive and learning strategies (Nieto Moreno de Diezmas, 2016), which are main components of learning to learn competence.

In the same vein, the aforementioned difficulty of conveying meaning in a language which is not the mother tongue of students and teachers leads to "widening of their teaching repertoires", (Ball, 2014, p. 77), usually including multimodal materials and digital resources, which scaffold students in this process. This way, "CLIL may indirectly help create favorable conditions for ICT integration" (Fernández Fontecha, 2012, p. 320), thereby contributing to acquiring another key competence, digital competence to a greater extent than mainstream education does (Nieto Moreno de Diezmas, 2018, 2021).

However, although there is evidence that CLIL settings provide more opportunities for curricular integration and a more competence-based approach, the specific integration of content and language learning, which is the crux of CLIL, remains an open issue. According to Coyle, Hood and Marsh (2010), in CLIL settings the integration of language and content is more systematically planned and taken into consideration by practitioners, especially when compared to immersion, where more attention to the role of integration in the learning process is needed (Genesee & Lindholm-Leary, 2013; Lyster, 2007).

Notwithstanding, these assumptions seem not to have been properly confirmed by research. Drawing upon Cenoz et al. (2014, p. 252) "evidence that there is a more balanced pedagogic integration of content and language in CLIL is scant". In the same vein, although the concept itself of "integrated learning" is included in the CLIL acronym, and integration is deemed to be an essential part of CLIL pedagogy, Nikula et al. (2016, p. 2) underscore that "operationalising such considerations to the more concrete level of research and educational practice still remains a challenge".

To put it briefly, it is needed to elaborate a more comprehensive theoretical construction on the concept of integration. Concomitantly, more studies taping on the process of integration in CLIL settings are necessary and undoubtedly teacher training programmes should focus on providing more attention to this capital issue. This is an urgent need, and therefore, the next section will be devoted to examining the main pedagogical frameworks underpinning and promoting the integrated learning of content and language in CLIL.

4.3 Pedagogical frameworks to enhance the integrated learning

Learning new contents delivered in a second language is a demanding process for students. To ease this cognitive load, Mehisto et al. (2008, p. 12) established a third element emerging in the duality of language and content: learning skills (Fig. 9). According to this triangle model, teachers should provide students with the necessary support and learning strategies to understand, classify, organise and process information so that learners can face the challenge the integrated language and content learning entails.

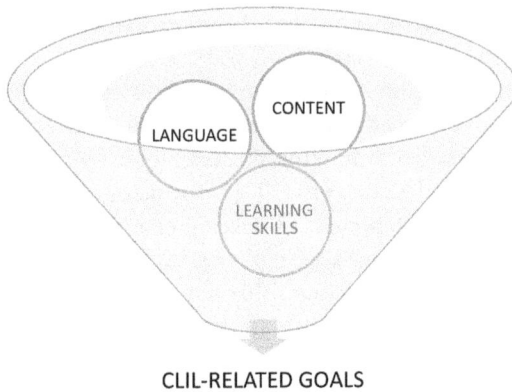

CLIL-RELATED GOALS

Fig. 9: CLIL-related goals. Source: Based on Mehisto et al. (2008, p. 12)

In the same lines, Coyle (1999) designed the well-known 4Cs Framework (communication, content, cognition and culture), drawing attention to the fact that in CLIL settings, the development of cognition (the third "c" of the framework) plays a crucial role in the integrated learning of content and communication. Along with "cognition" Coyle includes in the CLIL paradigm a fourth component: culture. Intercultural awareness, defined as the ability to establish connections among own cultural aspects, the culture of the target language, and other cultures, shapes multicultural competence and is an essential dimension of CLIL. Thus, these four elements configure the added value of CLIL. Therefore, according to Coyle (2011, p. 50), CLIL is "an approach to education which incorporates ways of using different languages in order to extend learner's cognitive, linguistic and cultural experiences" (Coyle, 2011, p. 50).

Coyle's 4 Cs framework has been revisited with the aim of considering another fundamental component, such as "community", which would be the fifth "c", which encompasses the crucial role that families and social contexts play in CLIL. In turn, Ball (2016) advocates the inclusion in the CLIL paradigm of another "c": competence, which refers to mobilisation of concepts, skills and attitudes to perform in real-life situations. As a result, "to be competent" should be at the core of the educational process. In the same vein, one step forward, we consider that the "c" to be added is "competences". With the incorporation of "competences", the conceptualisation of CLIL is more comprehensive and merges the European framework of the eight key competences for lifelong learning. As discussed in Section 4.2., the key competences are major educational goals and CLIL teachers should plan their lessons not only with language, content, cognition, and culture objectives in mind, but also considering the integral acquisition of the eight key competences (Fig. 8).

Coming back to the central role of thinking skills and cognition in CLIL settings, it is important to note that one of the most effective tools to develop cognition and work on students' thinking skills is Bloom's taxonomy in its revised version by Anderson and Krathwohl (2001). The taxonomy (Fig. 10) establishes a pyramid that displays the process of development from lower thinking skills (remembering, understanding, and applying) to higher order thinking skills (analysing, evaluating, and creating). This matrix helps teachers to plan their lessons and design activities to climb up this ladder, step by step, helping the students to acquire factual knowledge (recall basic concepts), conceptual knowledge (classify, interpret, organise), procedural knowledge (solve, perform), and metacognitive knowledge (strategic knowledge and self-knowledge). The ultimate goal is to equip students with the necessary tools to be able to create something new, and to train them to respond and creatively solve future situations in their adulthood.

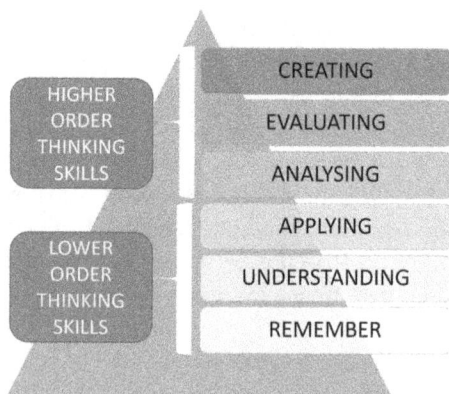

Fig. 10: Revised Bloom's taxonomy. Source: Based on Anderson and Krathwohl (2001)

To enable progression in the development of thinking skills, teachers should be able to organise adequate aids and scaffolds, especially in particularly challenging learning environments, as CLIL are, since the acquisition of contents, competences and learning thinking skills are mediated by and additional language, which also needs special treatment and support. To assist teachers in this task, the CLIL matrix (Cummins, 1984) is a very useful tool to identify the complexity of tasks in terms of both language and cognition demands (Fig. 11).

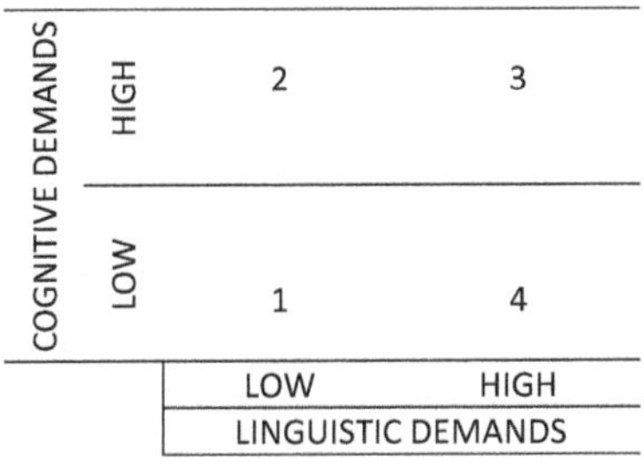

Fig. 11: CLIL matrix. Source: Based on Cummins (1984)

To interpret the CLIL matrix, it is important to bear in mind that tasks located in quadrant 1 are easy from the point of view of cognitive and linguistic effort and can provide a smooth starting point for the lessons, since they contribute to building confidence in students. Besides, according to constructivism, nothing new can be learnt if it is not connected with something that is already known. Thus, activities in quadrant 1 can activate previous knowledge and enable students to build knowledge by linking new concepts and skills in their existing knowledge structures and nets. On the opposite end, quadrant 3 comprises the tasks which are highly demanding both in terms of language and cognition, which means students need a lot of cognitive and language support to perform them. Otherwise, the task could be cognitively overwhelming and bring about a mental block. This type of tasks should be avoided, at least, during the first sessions of the lessons, until students have shown they are able to accomplish activities that are easier in terms of cognition (quadrant 4) or language (quadrant 2). Anyway, it is crucial to analyse cognitive and linguistic demands to avoid cognitive overload, and to get the necessary insight to carefully plan tailored scaffolding.

The concept of scaffolding is inscribed in the social constructivism theory (Vygotsky, 1978). This term is related to the assistance provided by the "more knowledgeable other" (MKO), i.e., educators, parents, or peers, in order to help learners move from what they already know and know to do, to the acquisition of new knowledge and skills. If the scaffolding is well-designed, students would be able to perform tasks they could not have done alone. Thanks to the practice and models that students get by means of the scaffolded activities, they will be eventually capable of accomplishing these tasks independently, which is the ultimate goal of the implementation of these teaching strategies. The process of scaffolding, as the process of learning itself, is developed in a social context and carried out by social interaction. As a result, teacher-student and student-student interactions are crucial and building blocks of learning when it comes to integrating content and language.

In addition to the frameworks and theories underpinning integrated learning, approaches such as task-based learning (TBL), project-based learning (PBL) and competence-based learning (CBL) provide learning environments which perfectly fit for CLIL needs and goals. These approaches are action-oriented and conducive to the mobilisation of concepts, skills, and attitudes in interdisciplinary scenarios, which is exactly what is needed in CLIL settings.

On the other hand, catering for diversity is the Achilles heel of education in general and for CLIL in particular. CLIL educators must face differences not only in terms of content levels of acquisition, learning styles, multiple intelligences, and motivation, but also regarding proficiency in the language of instruction. To accomplish what seems an impossible mission, scaffolding and variety are the keywords. Using a wide repertoire of teaching strategies and techniques and diverse materials and activities addressed to different learning styles and different multiple intelligence help students learn regardless of their dominant preference for a particular channel (visual, auditory or kinaesthetic) or intelligence (linguistic, logical, spatial, musical, interpersonal, intrapersonal, and naturalist). In turn, implementation of TBL, PBL and CBL provides scenarios in which students collaborative or individually can work according to their interests and abilities. Additionally, it is to be taken into account that CLIL students particularly need explicitly training in learning strategies, such as elaboration of graphic organisers, mnemonic technics, summaries, note-taking, text understanding and production strategies, etc.

Thus, the fact that school subjects are delivered in a second language, with the additional difficulties this scenario entails, pushes educators to implement enriched methodologies. In turn, to succeed in CLIL, students must make a double cognitive effort (Halbach, 2009) and develop their learning skills, thereby making a virtue out of necessity and becoming more effective learners (de Jabrun, 1997). In this vein, Dalton-Puffer considers (2008, p. 143) "rather than being a hindrance, L2 processing actually has a strong potential for the learning of subject-specific concepts". This optimistic outlook clashes with some accusations coming mostly from schools that have dropped the CLIL programme. In recent years, the media have been voicing these critics questioning the effectiveness of CLIL in guaranteeing the acquisition of contents and suggesting conceptual simplification and poor assimilation of knowledge is the norm and not the exception in CLIL programmes. In the next section these concerns will be addressed, in light of the research studies conducted in the field. It is of utmost importance for any educational innovation to guarantee the acquisition of the curriculum and CLIL is not an exception (Cf. 4.1).

4.4. Research on content outcomes: Main challenges of the integration under scrutiny

Despite negative narratives circulating particularly in Spain (see Bruton 2015, 2019), most of the empirical studies across different countries have shown the acquisition of content is satisfactory in the subjects taught through a second or additional language. Earliest investigations carried out to ascertain the effect of CLIL on content learning already concluded CLIL was not detrimental for content learning.

That was the case of the research conducted by Wode (1999) in German secondary schools. The outcomes of CLIL students were even higher than those of their non-CLIL peers in geography and history. Some years later, this time in Finland, the longitudinal study performed by Jäppinen (2005) with 669 participants revealed secondary school learners of mathematics and science showed similar acquisition of the matter content regardless the vehicular language (mother tongue or English). Also in Finland, Bergroth (2006) compared results of CLIL and non-CLIL students in the matriculation examination to access university students and found "immersion students as a group perform as well as or even better than their peers in regular programmes" (Bergroth, 2006, p. 132). The same outcome was reported in the Netherlands by Admiraal et al. (2006).

In turn, Stohler (2006, p. 41) conducted interviews to CLIL and non-CLIL students in secondary school in Switzerland and determined "the teaching of non-linguistic topics in a second language (L2) does not impair the acquisition of knowledge". One year later, also in Switzerland, Serra (2007) carried out a study set in primary school and identified that CLIL learners obtained even better results in mathematics than their non-CLIL peers. In Cyprus, Xanthou (2011) looked into acquisition of science contents in 6th graders when delivered in English and concluded that "findings seem to provide support for the positive impact of CLIL on content and L2 vocabulary development" (Xanthou, 2011, p. 124). In Spain, Madrid (2011) focused on social science performance in an *ad hoc* test based in the official curriculum of Andalusia conducted in CLIL and non-CLIL private and public schools. Results showed that in primary education, the CLIL branches outperformed the non-CLIL ones and differences between the CLIL private and the non-CLIL public schools were significant. However, in secondary education, the non-CLIL private schoolers significantly outperformed their CLIL counterparts in private and public schools. This finding suggest social science learning was robust in primary school CLIL settings, while in secondary school the contents of the official curricular were watered down.

In contrast, in Belgium, no negative effect of CLIL programmes, this time regarding mathematical competence, was detected (Surmont et al., 2016). The authors controlled by means of a test that CLIL and non-CLIL students had similar levels of mathematics before entering secondary school. Data revealed there were differences in favour of the students who incorporated into the CLIL group after 3 months, and these differences become significant 7 months later. This study indicates CLIL provided a more conducive scenario for acquiring and progressing in mathematical knowledge than mainstream education.

The same year, Anghel, Cabrales, and Carro (2016) published a study set in Madrid (Spain) with not so optimistic outcomes. The authors found no differences between primary school CLIL and non-CLIL learners in mathematics, which was delivered in the mother tongue for both groups. However, significantly lower outcomes were recorded in science by CLIL students who had studied science in English, compared to their mainstream counterparts who had taken it in their mother tongue (Spanish). In addition, the study showed that students with parents with lower cultural status were in a more disadvantageous situation in CLIL than in non-CLIL schools, in terms of learning outcomes. This finding is in accordance with the study conducted by Fernández-Sanjurjo et al. (2017) in Asturias (Spain), which corroborated students with low socioeconomic status scored particularly lower when enrolled in CLIL programmes. In addition, the authors evinced 6th grade primary school learners who were taught natural science in their mother tongue (Spanish) showed a better command in the contents of the subject than when those contents were delivered in English.

These negative effects of CLIL were, nevertheless, objected in the study carried out by Pérez Cañado (2018) who collected evidence from 2024 students of twelve Spanish monolingual provinces. The author made sure CLIL and non-CLIL groups were comparable in terms of verbal intelligence, motivation, and level of English. To ensure the homogeneity of the samples students were matched according to their scores in those aspects. This was done to avoid flaws in the research design existing in some preceding studies, thereby guaranteeing potential differences were not due to the hypothetical more advantageous previous predisposition of CLIL students. Results of the investigation ascertained that contrary to Fernández-Sanjurjo et al. (2017), CLIL students in primary education performed in natural science as well as their non-CLIL peers, and significantly better at the end of secondary school. In the same lines, with respect to primary education outcomes, Nieto Moreno de Diezmas and Hill (2019) guaranteed the homogeneity of the samples in terms of socioeconomic status and found no significant differences between CLIL and non-CLIL 4th graders performance in an *ad hoc* test based on the curricular contents already taught in both groups. An additional finding of this study evinced that there were no significant differences between boys and girls in the acquisition of science in CLIL programmes, whereas in mainstream education the boys recorded significantly higher scores than the girls. This outcome suggests CLIL exerted a positive effect on levelling gender-based differences in science competence. This finding is in keeping with the study by Nieto Moreno de Diezmas and García-Calvo (in press), which detected girls showed higher levels of motivation towards physical education when delivered in English than in mainstream programmes imparted in the mother tongue (in Spanish, in this case), in which boys were significantly more motivated than girls. All in all, although it seems that CLIL has an effect from a gender perspective, this assertion should be taken cautiously until more investigations tap into this new line of research.

Among the recent studies evincing CLIL assures the acquisition of contents, it is worth mentioning the longitudinal study carried out by San Isidro and Lasagabaster (2018), in Galicia (Spain) in secondary school. The homogeneity of the CLIL and non-CLIL groups was guarantee and it was confirmed the acquisition of social science knowledge was satisfactory for CLIL learners, who after two years in the programme, even outperformed their non-CLIL counterparts.

4.5. Future lines of study on content learning

All in all, most of the studies evinced contents were acquired to a similar or even to a greater extent in CLIL programmes. However, some issues concerning the content learning process remain open. Such is the case of the attention to diversity in CLIL settings. Some investigations distilled difficulties of students from socioeconomic disadvantaged backgrounds are not properly addressed in CLIL programmes, and that would be, definitely, an area in which there is room for improvement. However, this issue has already drawn scholars' attention by means of initiatives such as the ADiBE research project funded by the Spanish Ministry of Competitiveness, which aimed at designing and validating instruments to identify difficulties and best practices in catering for diversity in CLIL

(Pérez-Cañado et al., 2021) and collecting evidence in different European countries (Pérez-Cañado, 2021).

On the other hand, more research is needed to get more insight into the particularities of the integration process regarding different school subjects, with different disciplinary language and semiotics, and with diverse ways of expressing performance. In this vein, the integration has to adapt to the characteristics of the subject, since some disciplines are essentially procedural, such as art & crafts or physical education; others build more on language, as a vehicle for transmitting and expressing knowledge, such as social science and history, whereas subjects such as mathematics, physics and chemistry combine language with other semiotic systems.

Finally, the most conspicuous caveat to bring to the fore regarding studies on CLIL outcomes is that CLIL approach is flexible, and results of the investigations may vary just because they are looking into different contexts and practices which are nonetheless labelled under the CLIL umbrella. As a result, more research is needed to properly understand how particular differences in the design of the programmes may affect content learning.

Bibliography

Admiraal, W., Westhoff, G., & de Bot, K. (2006). Evaluation of bilingual secondary education in the Netherlands: Students' language proficiency in English. *Educational Research and Evaluation, 12,* 75–93. https://doi. org/10.1080/13803610500392160

Airey, J. (2012). I don't teach language. The linguistic attitudes of physics lecturers in Sweden. *AILA Review, 25,* 64–79. https://doi.org/10.1075/aila.25.05air

Airey, J. (2020). The content lecturer and English-medium instruction (EMI): Epilogue to the special issue on EMI in higher education. *International Journal of Bilingual Education and Bilingualism, 23*(39), 340–346. https://doi.org/10.1080/13670050.2020.1732290

Anderson, L. W., & Krathwohl, D. R. (Eds.). (2001). *A taxonomy for learning, teaching, and assessing: A revision of Bloom's taxonomy of educational objectives.* Longman.

Anghel, B., Cabrales, A., & Carro, J. M. (2016). Evaluating a bilingual education program in Spain: The impact beyond foreign language learning. *Economic Inquiry, 54*(2), 1202–1223. https://doi.org/10.1111/ecin.12305

Ball, Ph. (2014). CLIL and competences: Assessment. In Authors, *CLIL policy and practice: Competence-based education for employability, mobility and growth* (pp. 76–80). British Council.

Ball, Ph. (2016). Using language(s) to develop subject competences in CLIL-based practice. *Pulso, 39*, 15–34.

Bergroth, M. (2006). Immersion students in the matriculation examination three years after immersion. Exploring dual-focussed education. In S. Björklund, K. Mard- Miettinen, M. Bergström & M. Södergard (Eds.), *Integrating language and content for individual and societal needs* (pp. 123–134). www.uwasa.fi/materiaali/pdf/isbn_952-476-149-1.pdf

Bruton, A. (2015). CLIL: Detail matters in the whole picture. More than a reply to J. Hüttner and U. Smit (2014). *System, 53*, 119–128. https://doi.org/10.1016/j.system.2015.07.005

Bruton, A. (2019). Questions about CLIL which are unfortunately still not outdated: A reply to Pérez-Cañado. *Applied Linguistics Review, 10*(4), 591–602. https://doi.org/10.1515/applirev-2017-0059

Cenoz, J. (2015). Content-based instruction and content and language integrated learning: The same or different? *Language, Culture and Curriculum, 28*(1), 8–24. https://doi.org/10.1080/07908318.2014.1000922

Cenoz, J., Genesee, F., & Gorter, D. (2014). Critical analysis of CLIL: Taking stock and looking forward. *Applied Linguistics, 35*(3), 243–262. https://doi.org/10.1093/applin/amt011

Clegg, J. (2014). The role of CLIL in developing language and cognitive skills in the curriculum. In *CLIL policy and practice: Competence-based education for employability, mobility and growth* (pp. 83–94). British Council.

Coyle, D. (1999). Supporting students in content and language integrated contexts: Planning for effective classrooms. In J. Masih (Ed.), *Learning through a foreign language – models, methods and outcomes* (pp. 46–62). Centre for Information on Language Teaching and Research (CILT).

Coyle, D. (2011). Post-method pedagogies: Using a second or other language as a learning tool in CLIL settings. In Y. Ruiz de Zarobe, J. Sierra, & F. Gallardo del Puerto (Eds.), *Content and foreign language integrated learning* (pp. 49–74). Peter Lang.

Coyle, D., Hood, P., & Marsh, D. (2010). *Content and language integrated learning.* Cambridge University Press.

Cummins, J. (1984). *Bilingualism and special education: Issues in assessment and pedagogy.* Multilingual Matters.

Dalton-Puffer, C. (2008). Outcomes and processes in content and language integrated learning (CLIL): Current research from Europe. In W. Delanoy & L. Volkmann (Eds.), *Future perspectives for English language teaching* (pp. 139–157). Carl Winter.

Dalton-Puffer, C., Nikula, T., & Smit, U. (2010). Charting policies, premises and research on content and language integrated learning. In Ch. Dalton-Puffer, T. Nikula, & U. Smit (Eds.), *Language use and language learning in CLIL Classrooms* (pp. 1–22). John Benjamin Publishing.

Dalton-Puffer, C., & Smit, U. (2007). Introduction. In C. Dalton-Puffer & U. Smit (Eds.), *Empirical perspectives on CLIL classroom discourse*. Peter Lang.

De Jabrun, P. (1997). Academic achievement in late partial immersion French. *Babel*, *32*(2), 20–3.

European Commission. (2006). Recommendation of 18 December 2006 of the European Parliament and the Council on Key Competences for lifelong learning. Official Journal of the European Union L394.

European Commission. (2019). *Key competences for lifelong learning*, Publications Office. https://data.europa.eu/doi/10.2766/291008

Fernández-Sanjurjo, J., Fernández-Costales, A., & Arias Blanco, J. M. (2017). Analysing students' content-learning in science in CLIL vs. non-CLIL programmes: Empirical evidence from Spain. *International Journal of Bilingual Education and Bilingualism*. http://dx.doi.org/10.1080/1367005 0.2017.1294142.

Fernández Fontecha, A. (2012). CLIL in the foreign language classroom: Proposal of a framework for ICT materials design in language-oriented versions of content and language integrated learning. *Alicante Journal of English Studies*, *25*, 317–334. https://doi.org/10.14198/raei.2012.25.22

Fogarty, R. (1991). *The mindful school: How to integrate the curricula*. Skylight.

Genesee, F., & Lindholm-Leary, K. (2013). Two case studies of content-based language education. *Journal of Immersion and Content-Based Education*, *1*, 3–33. https://doi.org/10.1075/jicb.1.1.02gen

Halbach, A. (2009). The primary school teacher and the challenges of bilingual education. In E. Dafouz & M. C. Guerrini (Eds.), *CLIL across educational levels* (pp. 19–26). Richmond Publishing.

Humphreys, A., Post, T., & Ellis, A. (1981). *Interdisciplinary methods: A thematic approach*. Goodyear Publishing Company.

Ikeda, M., Izumi, S., Watanabe, Y., Pinner, R., & Davis, M. (2021). *Soft CLIL and English language teaching: Understanding Japanese policy, practice and implications*. Routledge.

Jäppinen, A. K. (2005). Thinking and content learning of mathematics and science as cognitional development in content and language integrated learning (CLIL): Teaching through a foreign language in Finland. *Language and Education*, *19*(2), 147–168. https://doi.org/10.1080/09500780508668671

Lyster, R. (2007). *Learning and teaching language thought content*. John Benjamins.

Madrid, D. (2011). Monolingual and bilingual students' competence in social science. In D. Madrid & S. Hughes (Eds.), *Studies in bilingual education* (pp. 195–222). Peter Lang.

Marsh, D., & Langé, G. (2000). *Using languages to learn and learning to use languages*. University of Jyväskylä.

Massler, U., Stotz, D., & Queisser, C. (2014). Assessment instruments for primary CLIL: The conceptualisation and evaluation of test tasks. *The Language Learning Journal, 42*, 137–150. https://doi.org/10.1080/09571736.2014.891371

Mehisto, P., Marsh, D., & Frigols, M. J. (2008). *Uncovering CLIL, content and language integrated learning in bilingual and multilingual education*. Macmillan.

Met, M. (1998). Curriculum decision-making in content-based language teaching. In J. Cenoz & F. Genesee (Eds.), *Beyond bilingualism: Multilingualism and multilingual education* (pp. 35–63). Multilingual Matters.

Nieto Moreno de Diezmas, E. (2016). The impact of CLIL on the acquisition of the learning to learn competence in secondary school education in the bilingual programmes of Castilla-La Mancha. *Porta Linguarum, 25*(1), 21–34. https://doi.org/10.30827/Digibug.53886

Nieto Moreno de Diezmas, E. (2018). Exploring CLIL contribution towards the acquisition of cross-curricular competences: A comparative study on digital competence development in CLIL. *Revista de lingüística y lengua aplicadas, 13*, 75–85. http://dx.doi.org/10.4067/S0718-48832018000200013

Nieto Moreno de Diezmas, E. (2021). Are CLIL settings more conducive to the acquisition of digital competences? A comparative study in primary education. In M. L. Pérez Cañado (Ed.), *Content and language integrated learning in monolingual settings: New insights from the Spanish context* (pp. 53–70). Springer International Publishing. https://doi.org/10.1007/978-3-030-68329-0_4 978-3-030-68328-3

Nieto Moreno de Diezmas, E., & Fernández Barrera, A. (2021). Main challenges of EMI at the UCLM: Teachers' perceptions on language proficiency, training and incentives. *Alicante Journal of English Studies, 34*, 39–61. https://doi.org/10.14198/raei.2021.34.02

Nieto Moreno de Diezmas, E., & García-Calvo, S. (in press). Educación Física Bilingüe-AICLE a través de la enseñanza comprensiva de los juegos: análisis comparativo de la satisfacción intrínseca por edad y género. *Retos*.

Nieto Moreno de Diezmas, E., & y Hill, T. M. (2019). Social Science learning and gender-based differences in CLIL. A preliminary study. *Estudios de lingüística inglesa aplicada (ELIA), 19*, 177–204. http://dx.doi.org/10.12795/elia.2019.i19.08

Nikula, T., Dalton-Puffer, C., Llinares, A., & Lorenzo, F. (2016). More than content and language: The complexity of integration in CLIL and bilingual education. In T. Nikula, E. Dafouz, P. Moore, & U. Smit (Eds.), *Conceptualising integration in CLIL and multilingual education* (pp. 1–26). Multilingual matters. https://doi.org/10.21832/9781783096145-004

Pérez Cañado, M. L. (2018). The effects of CLIL on L1 and content learning: Updated empirical evidence from monolingual contexts. *Learning and Instruction, 57*, 18–33. https://doi.org/10.1016/j.learninstruc.2017.12.002

Pérez Cañado, M. L. (2021). Inclusion and diversity in bilingual education: A European comparative study. *International Journal of Bilingual Education and Bilingualism*, 1–17. https://doi.org/10.1080/13670050.2021.2013770

Pérez Cañado, M. L., Rascón Moreno, D., & Cueva López, V. (2021). Identifying difficulties and best practices in catering to diversity in CLIL: Instrument design and validation. *International Journal of Bilingual Education and Bilingualism*, 1–9. https://doi.org/10.1080/13670050.2021.1988050

San Isidro, X., & Lasagabaster, D. (2018). The impact of CLIL on pluriliteracy development and content learning in a rural multilingual setting: A longitudinal study. *Language Teaching Research.* https://doi. org/10.1177/ 1362168817754103

Serra, C. (2007). Assessing CLIL at primary school: A longitudinal study. *International Journal of Bilingual Education and Bilingualism, 10*, 582–602. https:// doi.org/10.2167/beb461.0

Stohler, U. (2006). The acquisition of knowledge in bilingual learning: An empirical study on the role of language in content learning. *Vienna English Working Papers (Views), 15*, 41–46.

Stryker, S., & Leaver, B. (1997). *Content-based instruction in foreign language education.* Georgetown University Press.

Surmont, J., Struys, E., Van Den Noort, M., & Van De Craen, P. (2016). The effects of CLIL on mathematical content learning: A longitudinal study. *Studies in Second Language Learning and Teaching, 6*(2), 319–337. https://doi. org/10.14746/ssllt.2016.6.2.7

Vygotsky, L. S. (1978). *Mind in society: The development of higher psychological processes.* Harvard University Press.

Wode, H. (1999). Language learning in European immersion classes. In J. Masih (Ed.), *Learning through a foreign language. Models, methods and outcomes* (pp. 16–25). Centre for Information on Language Teaching and Research.

Xanthou, M. (2011). The impact of CLIL on L2 vocabulary development and content knowledge. *English Teaching: Practique and Critique, 10*(4), 116–126.

Chapter 5. Research-based findings on development of the mother tongue in CLIL programmes

Abstract: This chapter aims at providing an overview of research on mother tongue development in CLIL settings. As it is well-known, immersion and integrated learning programmes are characterised by using an additional or second language (L2) for delivering curricular content. This way more school time is allocated to the exposure to the additional language, thereby providing wider and meaningful opportunities for language learning within school hours. Notwithstanding, increased curricular presence of the additional language comes with a proportional reduction of the use of the mother tongue or first language (L1) for the academic instruction. Against this backdrop, it is not surprising that acquisition of L1 for academic purposes was one of the first and foremost concerns in early total immersion programmes implemented in Canada, in which most of the school subjects are taught by means of the L2, and the L1 virtually disappears from the academic instruction during the first years of schooling. Although in CLIL programmes, the number and proportion of the school subjects taught through the target language is usually not so high, in recent years, practitioners and families have expressed their concern about the acquisition of scientific terminology and academic proficiency in the mother tongue. CLIL researchers, after focusing mainly on measuring additional language learning outcomes, have turned their attention to this issue and undertaken empirical studies to determine whether CLIL might be detrimental for the development of the mother tongue.

In this chapter quantitative studies on mother tongue acquisition in immersion and CLIL programmes are expounded, in order to analyse the impact of these approaches in the development of literacy (reading and writing) in the L1. Age and educational level of students are the most relevant variables taken into account, since findings seem to indicate that there is an evolution from primary to secondary school learners, in terms of proficiency in literacy in L1. Results are discussed drawing upon theories such as language interdependence theory, transfer across languages, and CUP (Common Underlying Proficiency).

The last section of the chapter is devoted to critically provide with pedagogical guidelines concerning the role of languages in CLIL. Ways of reinforcement of the academic use of the mother tongue in CLIL programmes, and scaffolding techniques in the CLIL classroom (translanguaging and code-switching, among others) are addressed.

Keywords: Mother tongue development, bilingual education, immersion, multiliteracies, linguistic interdependence

5.1. Acquisition of literacy in the L1 in immersion programmes: The paradigm of Canada

Nowadays proficiency in two or more languages is widely deemed to be an asset for individuals to move up the success ladder. For families all around the world to raise "bilingual" children or provide them with enriched bi-multilingual learning environments is an aspiration, and against this backdrop, bilingual education is considered "as emblem of prestige, elitism and social distinction" (Relaño-Pastor & Fernández Barrera, 2018, p. 292).

However, before the 1960s, bilingualism was not so positively connoted, since as reported by Cummins (1979, p. 223), it was argued in the specialised literature that bilingualism "was a cause of mental confusion and language handicaps" and learning in a second language inevitably led to sacrifice a perfect acquisition of the L1 and entailed retardation in the assimilation of contents (Macnamara, 1966). Even the UNESCO (1953, p. 11) supported these standpoints, establishing that "it is axiomatic that the best medium for teaching a child is his mother tongue". These narratives caused experiences of immersion and bilingual education in Canada and US were embraced with caution, considering that in both cases the L2 used for instruction was a "weaker language", which could jeopardise the acquisition of the societal language (Macnamara, 1966).

Within this backdrop, from the very outset of the development of studies on immersion programmes in Canada, investigations were devoted to look into the acquisition of literacy, which was deemed to be a major concern. For researchers and stakeholders involved in immersion programmes, preservation of the mother tongue (English) was even more important than checking enhanced proficiency in the immersion language, i.e., the language used in the instruction of school subjects (in this case, French). Incidentally, this focus on mother tongue's safeguard widely differs from the CLIL research panorama, since most of the studies on CLIL were primarily and consistently addressed to determine target language learning outcomes (cf. 5.3). This divergence between immersion and CLIL critical research goals is ascribed to the fact that in immersion programmes the percentage of school subjects which are delivered through the L2 is substantially higher. In fact, in early total immersion programmes, during the first school years, the L2 is the language of instruction for 100% of the school time, which means that the mother tongue is practically banned from the academic context of the school.

It is paramount to note that concerns arise because literacy is acquired not only in the classroom of language arts but "either directly or indirectly, explicitly or implicitly, consciously or not, all subjects contribute to the development of reading competence" (Nieto Moreno de Diezmas, 2018, p. 44). With the decrease of school subjects taught in the L1, the academic exposure to the L1 and the opportunities to extent literacy competences in the L1, consequently would diminish. Having this situation in mind, early total immersion programmes were the first under scrutiny, since the exclusion of the mother tongue as the language of instruction is even total during the first years of schooling, as shown in Tab. 3.

Tab. 3: Time in L2 and L1 per week in early total immersion programmes

Grade	% L2 (French)	% L1 (English)
Kinder-garten	100 %	0 %
Grade 1	100 %	0 %
Grade 2	100 %	0 %
Grade 3	85 %	15 %
Grade 4	70 %	30 %
Grade 5	50 %	50 %
Grade 6	50 %	50 %

Source: Based on Genesee (2004)

Nevertheless, according to the investigations conducted during the first two decades after the inception of the early total immersion programmes, no negative effects were overall observed in the acquisition of literacy in the mother tongue, and "students in bilingual programmes … usually develop the same levels of proficiency in all aspects of the L1 as comparable students in programmes where the L1 is the exclusive medium of instruction" (Genesee, 2004, p. 553). However, studies did detect that immersion learners lagged behind in English word knowledge and reading comprehension tests in grade 3, when they had hardly been provided with instruction in English (Genesee, 1978, Lambert & Tucker, 1972; Swain & Lapkin, 1982). Notwithstanding, this initial disadvantage is very soon overcome, since after one of two years of receiving direct instruction of the mother tongue by means of the English language arts subject, the results of immersion students in vocabulary and reading comprehension were comparable to their non-immersion peers who had English as the language for instruction during all their schooling (Genesee, 1978, Lambert & Tucker, 1972; Swain & Lapkin, 1982). In higher grades immersion students continued performing as well as their counterparts.

A second surge of studies carried out in the 2000s revealed even more optimistic findings. Turnbull et al. (2001) used curriculum-based official tests developed by the regional office of evaluation (EQAO, Education Quality and Accountability Office of Ontario) and unveiled that in grade 3, immersion students had a higher level of English reading comprehension than non-immersion learners. 55 % of the students in French immersion programmes scored in level 3 (acceptable), and 4 (more than acceptable), whereas the percentage of students in regular programmes in these levels was lower, 48 %. As for reading competence in L1 in grade 6, Lapkin et al. (2003) found differences in favour of the immersion branch increased, since 71 % of French immersion students performed in levels 3 or 4 in comparison to only 51 % of students in English-only programmes. These differences could not be ascribed to socioeconomic status, since "immersion and English programme students were comparable with respect to socioeconomic background, ruling out this as an explanatory factor" (Genesee & Jared, 2008, p. 141). All in all, these investigations showed that early total immersion not only did not compromise the acquisition of literacy in the mother tongue but enhanced it.

Interestingly, it was also confirmed that early partial immersion programmes, in which there is more English instruction in the first years of schooling than in total immersion did not guarantee better results in reading in English. Similarly, delayed immersion programmes, in which the used of the L2 for the instruction of school subjects is introduced in the middle school or after, did not provide either better standards in reading comprehension in the L1 than early total immersion (Genesee, 2004; Genesee & Jared, 2008).

5.2. Lessons learnt from the Canadian immersion experience on mother tongue acquisition

The studies conducted in Canada surprisingly refuted the more-English-is-better hypothesis when English is the mother tongue. The acquisition of reading skills and vocabulary in English was not jeopardised in early total immersion despite its very limited presence in school time. Besides, other types of immersion programmes, such as early partial or late immersion, which provided a higher percentage of English at school, did not contribute more than early total immersion to enhance English reading comprehension.

At this point, some explanations emerge. In the first place, although during the first years of schooling, English was not used for the instruction, the competence of French immersion students in English reading "may also reflect student's literacy experiences outside school" (Genesee & Jared, 2008:), and it cannot be overlooked that "these students are exposed to the L1 on a daily basis outside school – at home, in the community, in the media, etc." (Genesee, 2004, p. 553). In a nutshell, acquisition of the societal language is not at risk in immersion programmes, since students are intensively exposed to it, when participating in a wide range of social interactions outside school, which includes contact with the written language.

On the other hand, most studies detected a lag in reading comprehension in L1 in grade 3, before the subject of English language was introduced in the curriculum. However, very quickly, within 1 or 2 years, they achieved parity and even outperformed their counterparts who received instruction exclusively in English. This rapid ability to catch up to non-immersion learners was ascribed to the existence of transfer of skills between languages (Cashion & Eagan, 1990), and, as a result, the academic skills acquired in the L1 and L2 are interdependent (Cummins, 1981). Thus, according to the linguistic interdependence principle, stated by Cummins (1981, p. 29): "to the extent that instruction in Lx is effective in promoting proficiency in Lx, transfer of this proficiency to Ly will occur provided there is adequate exposure to Ly (either in school or environment) and adequate motivation to learn Ly". This means that language skills and strategies acquired in one language can be transferred to another and vice versa. For example, if a student learns to identify main ideas of a text or deduce the meaning of unknown words using the context, these skills learnt in the L2 or in the L1 are valid in both languages. Thus, the linguistic transfer of strategies can occur from the immersion language to the mother tongue and the other way round.

The linguistic transfer is connected to the interdependence principle or interdependence hypothesis (Cummins, 1979), which works between any L1 and L2, although stronger cross-lingual correlations are observed between similar than dissimilar languages (Genesee, 1987). In this vein, more interrelations are observed between languages which belong to the same family, por example, Spanish and French, than between languages than are not so closely related, such as Japanese-English, Dutch-Turkish, etc., even if correlations and linguistic transfers are still operated when learning these languages.

The transfer of literacy-related skills and cognitive strategies are explained because of the existence of a common underlying proficiency (CUP). Although there are visible differences among languages in terms of pronunciation, vocabulary or grammar, there is a common stem which contains knowledge and strategies which can be acquired and applied across languages (Cummins, 1981). The CUP explains bilingual acquisition of literacy and is often depicted with the analogy of a dual iceberg (Fig. 12) with a shared base (Cummins, 1981). The dual iceberg represents that visible appearance of languages (the surface of the icebergs) is different, but there is a significant submerged part common to languages which acts as a language core operating system.

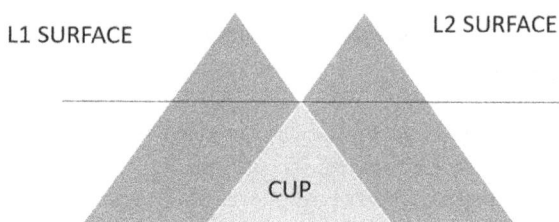

L1 SURFACE   L2 SURFACE

CUP

Fig. 12: The dual iceberg. Source: Based on Cummins (1979)

5.3. Literacy development in L1 in CLIL: The case of maximal L2 input settings

Contrary to research on immersion, aimed at dissipating concerns on the acquisition of literacy in the L1, the main drive of CLIL research was, from the beginning, to determine the effectiveness of the approach to improve proficiency in the target language, leaving aside other overriding areas, such as L1 and content learning (Lasagabaster & López-Beloqui, 2015). Already in 2005, Wolff includes the language competence in the mother tongue among the "controversial issues related to the learner in a CLIL learning context" (Wolff, 2005, p. 17). However, L1 continues being to date an under-researched aspect of CLIL programmes (Pérez Cañado, 2018, Nieto Moreno de Diezmas, 2020a, 2020b), and is still an area which "deserves further scrutiny" (Sierra et al., 2011, p. 320).

Pioneering studies exploring literacy in L1 in CLIL programmes were conducted in contexts with a high percentage of school time devoted to instruction of curricular subjects in the L2. That was the case of Belgium and Finland, where CLIL programmes provided between 50 and 75 % of school time delivered in a L2, with the consequent reduction of the academic exposure to the L1.

In the complex Belgian language scenario, divided into French speaking Wallonia and Dutch speaking Flanders, bilingual education emerged as a solution to bridge both communities and provide enhanced learning of Dutch in bilingual schools in Wallonia and French, in Flanders. The most researched programmes in Belgium were the ones implemented in Wallonia, where French is the majority societal language and the target language is Dutch, used for the instruction, around 50–75 % of the school time. Studies confirmed largely findings recorded in Canadian immersion programmes. De Samblanc (2006), Lecocq et al. (2004) and Van-de-Craen et al., (2007) compared reading and writing competence in French (the L1) of students taught entirely in French with students who had received about 50–75 % of the curriculum in Dutch, and differences, if any, were in favour of the bilingual group. Again, the societal language is not compromised because its learning is guarantee inside and outside school.

A subsequent study conducted by Van-de-Craen et al. (2010) ascribed the good command in the L1 of students in Dutch bilingual programmes to the literacy learning process. Although the L1 of these students was French, they were taught to read and write in Dutch and, after that, literacy in French was introduced. According to the authors (Van-de-Craen et al., 2010), it was simpler for learners to acquire literacy in Dutch, because of its high level of spelling-sound correspondence. After that, the way is paved for acquiring literacy in French, language in which correlations between letters and sounds is not so high, and consequently, decoding is more complex. Thus, interestingly, the strategy used for educators is starting literacy in the L2 (Dutch), which is "the easy language" in terms of decoding, and then continuing with literacy in the L1 (French), which despite being the mother tongue, it is considered to be a "difficult language" (French). The language learning principles which underpin this procedure are in connection with the theories of transfer, interdependence and CUP stated by Cummins in the context of Canadian immersion, which consider that decoding strategies necessary to read, acquired in Dutch, are available to be applied to reading in French.

Finland is another interesting setting for CLIL implementation and research. Despite the high amount of school time imparted in English (L2), no detrimental effects were found in the development of the mother tongue. For example, Bergroth (2006) investigated the impact of CLIL in the acquisition of written skills in the L1. To do this, the researcher compared the results of CLIL and non-CLIL students in the composition test of the matriculation examination students take in the end of secondary education. Results showed CLIL students performed as well or even better that their non-CLIL counterparts.

In turn, Seikkula-Leino (2007) was interested in ascertaining whether CLIL could affect students' achievement in L1 according to their cognitive capacities. The sample of the study was made up of grades 5 and 6 non-CLIL and CLIL learners who received between 40 and 70 % of instruction in English. To determine the measures of intelligence of students, the author used Raven's non-verbal intelligence test and Wechsler's vocabulary test. This result was compared with the marks obtained in Finnish language, and students were classified into overachievers (their marks were above their capability) underachievers (with marks below their potential) and achievers (with an adequate relation between their marks and their intelligence). Results indicated that CLIL programmes exerted no effect in overachieve, achieve, or underachieve in L1, i.e., no differences were found between both cohorts in getting marks under, below or in line with their capability.

Merisuo-Storm's (2006) conducted a longitudinal study to compare CLIL and non-CLIL learners in grades 1 and 2 of primary education regarding the acquisition of literacy in their L1. In this case, 20% of the sessions were delivered in English, which is an amount substantially lower than in the programme researched by Seikkula-Leino (2007). Results showed that the CLIL group already significantly outperformed the non-CLIL group at the beginning of first grade, and these differences were maintained after 2 years. Interestingly, students with a poor or excellent starting level of literacy progressed in a similar way regardless they were in the CLIL or in the non-CLIL classes.

Likewise, this time in the Netherlands, Admiraal et al. (2006) studied the potential detrimental effects for L1 development in CLIL students who had received around 50 % of the curriculum in English during compulsory secondary education and had to take in Dutch (their mother tongue) their final tests to access university studies. Findings indicated no difference between CLIL and non-CLIL students in those exams. As a result, the bilingual programme had helped learners acquire higher levels of English proficiency and had preserved desirable performance in their L1.

5.4 The case of Spain: Mother tongue and CLIL in bilingual and monolingual settings

Although, already in 2010, it was considered that Spain, was "rapidly becoming one of the European leaders in CLIL practice and research" (Coyle, 2010, p. viii), its linguistic panorama is, to say the least, intricate (see Tab. 1). Spanish is the national official language in the seventeen Autonomous Communities and the two Autonomous Cities of Ceuta and Melilla. Besides, in six of these autonomous communities there is another co-official language: Catalan, Galician or Basque. In these bilingual autonomous communities, the heritage languages are also being used for the instruction of academic subjects in all educational levels, in different proportions depending on the territory and the linguistic programme. Additionally, CLIL programmes are currently running to provide instruction in foreign languages (mainly English), to enhance multilingualism and foreign languages learning.

In the Basque Country, a bilingual autonomous community, Merino and Lasagabaster (2018) conducted a longitudinal study with 285 secondary school learners. Reading comprehension and written production development in the two co-official languages, Basque and Spanish of CLIL and non-CLIL students were compared over a year. Non-CLIL students received 75.9 % of school time in Basque, 12.9 % in Spanish and 11.3 % in English (exclusively in the English language subject). The percentages of these three languages for the CLIL group were: 63 % Basque; 14.4 % Spanish and 22.5 % English (in the English language subject plus in a content subject). Results indicated that CLIL students significantly outperformed their non-CLIL peers in writing production, and their progress over a year was also statistically significant. No significant differences were detected in reading comprehension and this competence evolved similarly in both groups. Regarding Basque, the CLIL group obtained higher outcomes in reading and writing and both groups showed a similar development one year later.

All in all, English instruction by means of CLIL did not hinder acquisition of Basque and Spanish. According to the authors, this conclusion is to take with caution, since the CLIL programme subtracted only 3–4 sessions from the instruction in Basque to devote them to deliver one content subject in English. With more subjects in English, the acquisition of Basque, the minority language could be at risk, which was a fear, -to date unfounded-, already expressed in previous studies (Cenoz, 2009; Lasagabaster & Sierra, 2009). The authors suggest more research is needed to ascertain the way these three languages complement each other instead or compete among them. Maybe one of the explanations to this harmonious language development has to do with the potential of multilingualism to enhance positive attitudes towards language learning and towards all the languages in contact, as it was detected in the same research setting as an additional effect of CLIL (Lasagabaster & Sierra 2009).

In Galicia, with two co-official languages, Spanish and Galician, San Isidro and Lasagabaster (2018) explored the development of both languages in CLIL and non-CLIL students over a 2-year span in a secondary school, and their results were in keeping with Merino and Lasagabaster's (2018). Thus, the authors concluded that minimising the exposure to the minority language (Galician) in favour of instruction in English did not entail a detrimental effect for its acquisition. Even, over the 2 years, CLIL students improved in Galician and Spanish to a greater extent than the non-CLIL group. The authors acknowledged this finding could be ascribed to the specific training teachers received and the multilingual approach implemented in the CLIL programme based on common work in the three languages. Lesson plans were designed considering interdependence among languages, which were "approached from a holistic perspective" (San Isidro & Lasagabaster, 2018, p. 15).

In the thirteen monolingual autonomous communities of Spain, CLIL programmes are also being implemented since around mid-2000s. The studies carried out to assess L1 development are also few in this context, but unanimously confirmed CLIL was not overall detrimental to literacy in L1, particularly in the long run, when CLIL students even significantly outperformed their non-CLIL peers. This trend has been particularly identified in four large-scale studies conducted in central Spain (Nieto Moreno de Diezmas, 2017, 2018, 2020a, b), which investigated reading and writing in primary and secondary school in the CLIL programme launched by the education administration of Castilla- La Mancha. The studies collected data from the five provinces of the region and their findings are discussed below.

Regarding reading comprehension in primary school, no differences were found between CLIL and non-CLIL students in grade 4 when the literal and inferential levels of reading competence in their mother tongue (Spanish) were assessed. Even CLIL students scored significantly higher in "receptive vocabulary", one of the aspects integrating the literal reading level. However, CLIL learners did lag significantly behind in critical reading. As a result, a detrimental effect of CLIL was identified in 9–10-year-olds. This might be attributed to the fact that CLIL content teachers were possibly more focused on exercising literal and inferential levels of reading, which would enable students to deal with academic matter comprehension, than on preparing them to critically read texts (Nieto Moreno de Diezmas, 2018).

Notwithstanding, this specific negative effect is no longer detected in four years older CLIL secondary school students in the study conducted looking into the same CLIL programme in the same territory (Nieto Moreno de Diezmas, 2017). The competence of CLIL secondary school students in the critical reading comprehension level was similar to their non-CLIL peers. Besides, CLIL students not only caught up to their partners entirely educated in their L1 in critical reading, but also significantly outperformed them in the literal and inferential reading comprehension levels. These results seem to mirror the findings of studies conducted in Canadian immersion programmes, since in the first years of primary education, immersion students were behind their non-immersion peers in reading in L1, but one or two years later, they got parity in this regard (Genesee & Jared, 2008).

As for writing in L1, CLIL primary school learners scored lower than the non-CLIL counterparts, but differences were not significant (Nieto Moreno de Diezmas, 2020a). However, intriguingly, CLIL seemed to affect the development of certain skills positively and negatively. CLIL learners significantly outperformed non-CLIL ones in expressive richness and spelling but were significantly behind in planning strategies and use of text typology. When the same programme was evaluated in terms of written production in L1 in secondary school (Nieto Moreno de Diezmas, 2020b), CLIL students continued standing out for their expressive richness and spelling, but also statistically outperformed their counterparts in all the subskills considered: planning, text typology, vocabulary and grammar. Interestingly, the wider differences in favour of the CLIL group were detected in the areas of writing which resulted more complex, drawing upon the scoring of CLIL and non-CLIL students: spelling, planning and expressive richness. This finding is in keeping with previous studies which identified CLIL students tended to be particularly effective in the most challenging tasks (Pérez-Cañado & Lancaster, 2017; Prieto-Arranz et al., 2015). Results seemed to indicate that significant positive effects of CLIL are displayed in the medium or long term, and particularly in secondary education.

In line with the aforementioned studies conducted in secondary schools (Nieto Moreno de Diezmas, 2018, 2020b), Navarro-Pablo & López Gándara (2020) identified a significant advantage of CLIL secondary school students in L1, which also has been already detected even in primary school. The quantitative data was consistent with the impressions of teachers and students, who manifested CLIL promoted higher performance in L1 and more effective ways to understand how languages work, which positively impacted in the acquisition of both languages.

Within this framework, the study developed by Pérez-Cañado (2018) is without a doubt one of the most robust conducted in the area. The researcher analysed data coming from Extremadura, Andalusia, and the Canary Islands, (monolingual autonomous communities). Homogeneity between CLIL and non-CLIL groups was guaranteed with regards to motivation, verbal intelligence, and English level. The setting, the type of school, and socioeconomic status (SES) were considered intervening variables. Results showed CLIL students outperformed their non-CLIL peers in L1 in primary education and with a wider difference also in secondary education. However, discriminant analyses indicated that the differences were best explained by verbal intelligence and motivation in primary education, and by motivation in secondary school. Interestingly, the study revealed that there was a clear-cut urban/rural divide in L1 competence in non-CLIL settings, with urban non-CLIL students outperforming their rural counterparts. Surprisingly, CLIL seemed to display a leveller effect on these differences so that "CLIL learners perform equally well on the L1 at both educational stages considered, irrespective of the type of setting in which they are studying" (Pérez-Cañado, 2018, p. 24). Another overarching conclusion of this study is that students with a higher SES perform better in L1 than students with lower SES regardless they are in CLIL or non-CLIL programmes. This finding would dismiss CLIL would deploy a detrimental effect on the acquisition of L1 for students with low SES, since CLIL and non-CLIL programmes have the same effect on this aspect.

5.5. Final considerations: Pedagogical guidelines related to the role of languages in CLIL and future lines of work

The main conclusion to be drawn from the studies reviewed in the previous sections is that, in bilingual education programmes, the fact that a part of the curriculum is imparted in a L2 does not impoverishes L1 competence. This finding is pertinent for both immersion and CLIL programmes. L1 acquisition is guaranteed even in the most unfavourable milieux such as early total immersion programmes, in which the reduction of the L1 is dramatic during the first years of schooling (cf. Section 5.1), and CLIL provisions in territories where there are already two national languages (e.g., bilingual autonomous communities in Spain), and a third language (a foreign language that is usually English) is introduced for the academic instruction (cf. Section 5.4).

From a psychological point of view, the linguistic interdependence principle, stated by Cummins (1981), the transfer of general skills across languages, and the existence of a common substratum of language strategies and knowledge applicable to all language learning (CUP) account for the fact that limited instruction in the L1 does not hinder literacy in that language. These explanatory theories emerged in relation to Canadian immersion programmes but can be undoubtedly extrapolated to CLIL settings.

From a methodological perspective, further explanations arise. For example, CLIL is claimed to promote teachers' special attention to language scaffolding and awareness, and therefore, it provides "a good framework for language learning on a plurilingual basis" (San Isidro & Lasagabaster, 2018, p. 15). CLIL also seems to be conducive to the implementation of more holistic pedagogies, including specific awareness of interdependence among languages, implementation of common projects in the L1 and the L2 (and L3), and the design of structured plans based on the collaboration of the whole school to enhanced language learning across all subjects, such as centre language projects (Trujillo Saez, 2015).

Additionally, although most CLIL programmes determine that 100 % of the lessons of the CLIL subjects are to be imparted in the target language, it is being identified that L1 is more than present in the content instruction. In fact, Navarro-Pablo and López Gándara (2020), in their study conducted in the south of Spain, observed that both Spanish and English were used to deliver content in all classes, and the proportion of time allocated to Spanish was higher in primary schools than in secondary education. These translanguaging and mediation practices are implemented by teachers with sometimes a feeling that the ideal of exclusive use of the target language is not accomplished. However, translanguaging can be very useful to scaffold content comprehension (Karabassova & San Isidro, 2020) and acquisition of technical terms in the mother tongue (Nieto Moreno de Diezmas & Fernández Barrera, 2021). On the whole, more pedagogical guidelines seem to be needed in bilingual education programmes to determine and establish the role of the mother tongue in those settings, leaving aside counter-productive complexes.

This is an overriding issue that needs to be properly and more profusely addressed by stakeholders. Indeed, more investigations in this area are to be carried out to progress in knowledge and good practice on L1 development. Additionally, according to Pérez-Cañado (2020) the future research path forward on L1 should also include replicating and extending studies. This way more insight can be obtained into contextual needs, which would provide informed views to intervene in terms of teacher training. Furthermore, Pérez Cañado (2020) underscores the time is ripe to meta-analyse existing research, which can be useful to ascertain how CLIL is working and what patterns are common across different contexts.

Finally, it is critical to note that studies presented and discussed in this chapter are focused on the acquisition of the L1, but they have used instruments which are exclusively able to determine the acquisition of general literacy skills. For example, for reading comprehension, literary (narrations, descriptions, dialogues) or press (articles, reports) texts have been mostly used. For written production the participants usually had to perform different tasks, including correcting sentences and writing compositions about different general topics not strictly connected to the specific school subjects.

However, some of the narratives being heard in recent times question whether CLIL and bilingual education can guarantee the acquisition of academic concepts and scientific terms in L1 and, for instance, it is claimed students in bilingual programmes do not know how to name in their mother tongue the bones of the human body, the parts of a flower, or the elements of the periodic table. Against this backdrop, it is paramount to research the effect of bilingual education on academic language in the L1. Thus, future studies should precisely look into students' receptive and productive scientific vocabulary in L1 related to the specific subjects they are learning through the L2. As for writing, it should be assessed whether CLIL students can write academic texts in their L1 on the content matter they study in L2 as their non-CLIL counterparts do. This is a line of research that needs to be explored in order to get further insight into the acquisition of cognitive academic language proficiency (CALP) in L1 in CLIL settings and obtain food for thought on the potential pedagogical implications.

Bibliography

Admiraal, W., Westhoff, G., & de Bot, K. (2006). Evaluation of bilingual secondary education in The Netherlands: Students' language proficiency. *English Educational Research and Evaluation, 12,* 75–93. https://doi.org/10.1080/13803610500392160

Bergroth, M. (2006). Immersion students in the matriculation examination three years after immersion. In K. Björklund, M. Mård- Miettinen, M. Bergström, & M. Södergård (Eds.), *Exploring dual-focussed education, integrating language and content for individual and societal needs* (pp. 123–134). University of Vaasa.

Cashion, M., & Eagan, R. (1990). Spontaneous reading and writing in English by students in total French immersion: Summary of final report. *English Quarterly, 22*(1), 30–44.

Cenoz, J. (2009). *Towards multilingual education. Basque educational research from an international perspective.* Multilingual Matters. https://doi.org/10.21832/9781847691941

Coyle, Do. (2010). Foreword. In D. Lasagabaster & Y. Ruiz de Zarobe (Eds.), *CLIL in Spain: Implementation, results and teacher training* (pp. vii–viii). Cambridge Scholars Publishing.

Cummins, J. (1979). Linguistic interdependence and the educational development of bilingual children. *Review of Educational Research, 49*(2), 222–251. https://doi.org/10.2307/1169960

Cummins, J. (1981). The role of primary language development in promoting educational success for language minority students. In California State Department of Education (Ed.), *Schooling and language minority students: A theoretical framework*. Evaluation. Dissemination and Assessment Center, California State University, Los Angeles.

De Samblanc, G. (2006). *De immersiescholen in de Franse Gemeenschap. Lezing gehou den op de studiedag Meertaligheid en basisonderwijs*. Ministerie van onderwijs

Genesee, F. (1978). Is there an optimal age for starting second language instruction? *McGill Journal of Education, 13*, 145–154.

Genesee, F. (1987). *Learning through two languages: Studies of immersion and bilingual education*. Newbury House.

Genesee, F. (2004). What do we know about bilingual education for majority language students? In T. K. Bhatia & W. Ritchie (Eds.), *Handbook of bilingualism and multiculturalism* (pp. 547–576). Blackwell.

Genesee, F., & Jared, D. (2008). Literacy development in early French immersion programs. *Canadian Psychology, 49*(2), 140–147. https://doi.org/10.1037/0708-5591.49.2.140

Karabassova, L., & San Isidro, X. (2020). Towards translanguaging in CLIL: A study on teachers' perceptions and practices in Kazakhstan. *International Journal of Multilingualism*. https://doi.org/10.1080/14790718.2020.1828426

Lambert, W. E., & Tucker, G. R. (1972). *Bilingual education of children: The St. Lambert experience*. Rowley.

Lapkin, S., Hart, D., & Turnbull, M. (2003). Grade 6 French immersion students' performance on large- scale reading, writing, and mathematics tests: Building explanations. *Alberta Journal of Education, 49*, 6–23. https://doi.org/10.11575/ajer.v49i1.54956

Lasagabaster, D., & López Beloqui, R. (2015). The impact of type of approach CLIL *versus* EFL and methodology book-based *versus* project work on motivation. *Porta Linguarum, 23*(1), 41–57. https://doi.org/10.30827/Digibug.53737

Lasagabaster, D., & Sierra, J. M. (2009a). Immersion and CLIL in English: More differences than similarities. *ELT Journal, 63*(4), 367–375. https://doi.org/10.1093/elt/ccp082

Lasagabaster, D., & Sierra, J. M. (2009b). Language attitudes in CLIL and traditional EFL classes. *International CLIL Research Journal, 1*(2), 4–17.

Lecocq, K., Mousty, P., Kolinsky, R., Goetry, V., Morais, J., & Alegria, J. (2004). *Evaluation des programs d'immersion en communauté française: une étude longitudinale comparative du développement des compétences linguistiques d'enfants francophones immergés en néerlandais*. http://www.enseignement. be/index.php?page=26044&id_fiche=996&dummy=24855

Macarena Navarro, P., & López Gándara, Y. (2020). The effects of CLIL on L1 competence development in monolingual contexts. *The Language Learning Journal*, *48*(1), 18–35. https://doi.org/10.1080/09571736.2019.1656764

Macnamara, J. (1966). *Bilingualism and primary education*. Edinburg University Press.

Merino, J. A., & Lasagabaster, D. (2018). CLIL as a way to multilingualism. *International Journal of Bilingual Education and Bilingualism*, *21*(1), 79–92. https:// doi.org/10.1080/13670050.2015.1128386

Merisuo-Storm, T. (2006). Development of boys' and girls' literacy skills and learning attitudes in CLIL education. In S. Björklund, K. Mård-Miettinen, M. Bergström, & M. Södergård (Eds.), *Exploring dual-focussed education: Integrating language and content for individual and societal needs* (pp. 176–88). Centre for Immersion and Multilingualism, University of Vaasa.

Nieto Moreno de Diezmas, E. (2017). How does CLIL affect the acquisition of reading comprehension in the mother tongue? A comparative study in secondary education. *Investigaciones Sobre Lectura*, *8*(8), 7–26. https://doi.org/ 10.37132/isl.v0i8.214

Nieto Moreno de Diezmas, E. (2018). Adquisición de la lectura en L1 en programas bilingües de Educación Primaria. Un estudio comparativo. *Ocnos. Revista de estudios sobre lectura*, *17*, 43–54. http://orcid.org/0000-0001-8753-5857

Nieto Moreno de Diezmas, E. (2020a). Literacy Development in L1 in bilingual education: Evidence from research on CLIL in primary school. In M. Gómez-Parra & C. Huertas Abril (Eds.), *Handbook of research on bilingual and intercultural education* (pp. 383–407). IGI Global. https://doi.org/10.4018/ 978-1-7998-2588-3.ch016

Nieto Moreno de Diezmas, E. (2020b). Mother tongue development in bilingual programs type CLIL in secondary school: A comparative study on written production. *RLA. Revista De Lingüística Teórica Y Aplicada*, *58*(2), 117–136. https://doi.org/10.29393/RLA58-11MTEN10011

Nieto Moreno de Diezmas E., & Fernández Barrera A. (2021). Translanguaging and language mediation in EMI contexts: Emotional stances and translation issues. In L. Escobar & A. Ibáñez Moreno (Eds.), *Mediating specialized knowledge and L2 abilities* (pp. 17–34). Palgrave Macmillan. https://doi.org/ 10.1007/978-3-030-87476-6_2

Pérez Cañado, M. L. (2018). The effects of CLIL on L1 and content learning: Updated empirical evidence from monolingual contexts. *Learning and Instruction*, *57*, 18–33. https://doi.org/10.1016/j.learninstruc.2017.12.002

Pérez Cañado, M. (2020). What's hot and what's not on the current CLIL research agenda: Weeding out the non-issues from the real issues. A response to Bruton (2019). *Applied Linguistics Review.* https://doi.org/10.1515/appli rev-2020-0033

Pérez-Cañado, M. L., & Lancaster, N. (2017). The effects of CLIL on oral comprehension and production: A longitudinal case study. *Language, Culture, and Curriculum, 30*(3), 300–316. https://doi.org/10.1080/07908318.2017.1338717

Prieto-Arranz, J. I., Rallo Fabra, L., Calafat-Ripoll, C., & Catrain González, M. (2015). Testing progress on receptive skills in CLIL and non-CLIL contexts. In M. Juan-Garau & J. Salazar Noguera (Eds.), *Content-based language learning in multilingual educational environments* (pp. 123–137). Springer. https://doi.org/10.1007/978-3-319-11496-5_8

Relaño Pastor, A. M., & Fernández Barrera, A. (2018). Competing bilingual schools in La Mancha city: Teachers' responses to neoliberal language policy and CLIL practices. *Foro de Educación, 16*(25), 283–309. http://dx.doi.org/10.14516/fde.624

San Isidro, X., & Lasagabaster, D. (2018). The impact of CLIL on pluriliteracy development and content learning in a rural multilingual setting: A longitudinal study. *Language Teaching Research, 23*(5), 584–602. https://doi.org/10.1177/1362168817754103

Seikkula-Leino, J. (2007). CLIL learning: Achievement levels and affective factors. *Language and Education, 21*(4), 328–341. https://doi.org/10.2167/le635.0

Sierra, J. M., Gallardo del Puerto, F., & Ruiz de Zarobe, Y. (2011). Good practice and future actions on CLIL: Learning and Pedagogy. In Y. Ruiz de Zarobe, J. Sierra, & F. Gallardo del Puerto (Eds.), *Content and foreign language integrated learning: Contributions to multilingualism in European contexts* (pp. 317–338). Peter Lang.

Swain, M., & Lapkin, S. (1982). *Evaluating bilingual education: A Canadian case study.* Multilingual Matters.

Trujillo Sáez, F. (2015). Un abordaje global de la competencia lingüística. *Cuadernos de Pedagogía, 458*, 1–3.

UNESCO. (1953). *The use of vernacular languages in education.* Monographs on fundamental education.

Van-de-Craen, P., Mondt, K., Allain, L., & Gao, Y. (2007). Why and how CLIL works. An outline for a CLIL theory. *VIEWS Vienna English Working Papers, 18*(3), 70–7.

Van-de-Craen, P., Mondt, K., Ceuleers, E., & Migom, E. (2010). EMILE a douze ans. Douze ans d'enseignement de type immersif en Belgique. Résultats et perspectives. *SYNERGIES – Monde, 7*, 127–140.

Wolff, D. (2005). Approaching CLIL. In D. Marsh (Coord) (Ed.). *The CLIL quality matrix. Central workshop report.* http://www.ecml.at/mtp2/CLILmat rix/pdf/wsrepD3E2005_6.pdf

Part III. Preservice and inservice CLIL teacher training

Chapter 6. Critical analysis of initial teacher education for CLIL

Abstract: The theory and principles of CLIL, as well as its effects in practice, have been extensively studied. Regarding teacher education, efforts have also been made to provide a theoretical framework for CLIL (Mehisto et al., 2008; Coyle et al., 2010; Dale & Tanner, 2012; Ball et al., 2015; Ikeda et al., 2021), to design a CLIL teacher framework (Bentley, 2010; Bertaux et al., 2010; Marsh et al., 2010; Sasajima, 2019), and to define CLIL teachers' key competences (Marsh et al., 2010; Bertaux et al., 2010; Pérez-Cañado, 2017). However, the actual performance of CLIL teachers in their classrooms is still deficient and even lacks any kind of CLIL training (Custodio Espinar & García Ramos, 2019, 2020). In CLIL research studies, unfortunately, it is too frequent to read the conclusion "...lack of CLIL training for teachers". This reality is due to a combination of multiple factors likely to result in the current heterogenous scenario concerning CLIL teacher training and competence in CLIL.This chapter explores, from an international perspective, the actions taken by different institutions to meet the challenges of providing prospective CLIL teachers with the skills and competences necessary to implement this approach. The aim is to analyse the strengths and weaknesses of different actions and strategies for initial teacher preparation and to consider their potential to be transferred into other contexts. The chapter starts with the review of the actions taken by European universities as a result of the Bologna Process from two different perspectives: the adaptation of universities to the European Higher Education Area and how this has impacted the design of the degrees in Education; on the other hand, this paper attempts to explain the increasing offer of postgraduate studies in the so-called "bilingual education" and CLIL. Finally, the chapter deals with an important issue in teacher education, which is related to the difficulty of meeting the challenges and needs of different teacher profiles: i.e., language teacher, content teacher; at different levels, i.e., pre-primary, primary, secondary teacher; and in different contexts, i.e., state schools, semi-private schools, private schools. A multivariate analysis of preservice CLIL teachers in different countries is offered in the chapter to identify common areas of training needs for all that should be on the base of any CLIL teacher training programme at the undergraduate level, leaving postgraduate studies for specialisation.

Keywords: Bilingual education, student teachers, higher education, preservice teacher education, teacher educator training.

6.1. CLIL education at university

Mobility is one of the characteristics of 21st-century society. The Sorbonne Declaration in 1998 signed by four European countries (France, Germany, Italy and the United Kingdom) and the subsequent signing by thirty-one countries of the Bologna Declaration in 1999 are at the origin of the creation of the European Higher Education Area (EHEA)[4]. Since then, ministerial conferences are held every 2 or 3 years to assess the progress made within the EHEA and to decide on the new steps to be taken in the process of reforming higher education systems in European Union member states and beyond. These conferences are organised by the Bologna Follow-Up Group (BFUG)[5]. The current number of members is 48 (European Commission, 2020). This international collaboration on higher education has brought structural reforms to the higher education systems of the members to make them more compatible and to increase staff and students' mobility and facilitate employability.

The Work Plan 2021–24 includes a Working Group on Learning and Teaching, which is focused on the following topics (EHEA, 2022):

- Making student-centred learning a reality across the entire EHEA;
- Supporting staff development;
- Fostering innovative learning and teaching. These should ensure interdisciplinary, intersectoral and experiential learning as outcomes. Innovations in learning and teaching should also contribute to opening up higher education to lifelong and non-traditional learners, for example, through micro-credentials;
- Discussing assessment in higher education to encompass a wider set of learning outcomes, in addition to disciplinary knowledge, such as interdisciplinarity and transversal, green and digital competencies;
- Strengthening the capacity of higher education institutions and systems, to support the continuous improvement of learning, teaching and assessment;
- Developing international learning environments for the students, such as the inclusion of a mobility experience or access to internationalisation at home. (pp. 1–2)

---

4 https://education.ec.europa.eu/levels/higher-education/inclusion-connectivity/bolo gna-process-european-higher-education-area

5 http://ehea.info/page-the-bologna-follow-up-group

The context that transpires from this list of intentions opens a clear space for the inclusion of bilingual education and CLIL in higher education, which has been called ICLHE (integrating content and language in higher education) (Pavón-Vázquez & Gaustad, 2013; Smit & Dafouz-Milne, 2012). This chapter addresses the impact of this educational reform on higher education, specifically on the degrees of education and the provision of CLIL training that future teachers receive.

6.1.1 The repercussions of Bologna on the design of education degrees

Before Bologna, degree systems in the European Union were varied and diverse (European Commission, 2020). One of the most important advances that led to unifying these systems was the development of qualifications frameworks for the national education systems to be compatible with the three-cycle framework (bachelor, master, doctorate) adopted in 2005 by the EHEA (European Commission, 2020). In this process, the so-called Bologna Toolkit has supported the political commitments towards this reform to underpin its development. The three main tools developed are: The Diploma Supplement (DS); the European Credit Transfer and Accumulation System (ECTS); and the National qualifications frameworks (NQFs), aligned to a European framework to support structural reforms (p. 39).

In the case of Spain, the Order 3857/2007, 27th of December regulated the design of new teacher training degrees with the aim of aligning them to the EHEA (López-Hernández, 2021). This regulation meant a turn to more generalist training in the new EHEA degrees that has caused a reduction in the ECTS devoted to foreign language training (Custodio Espinar, 2019). As López-Hernández affirms, this is due to the creation of "a number of formative itineraries or tracks, called *menciones*, which offer significantly fewer modules and credits than the former specialised degrees, and tend to concentrate them in the last two years of students' training" (2021, p. 133). This panorama has led universities to employ "different models when implementing bilingual itineraries and preparing their teachers for its challenges" (Johnson, 2012, p. 72), and, in particular, between private and state universities in their initial teacher education (ITE) programmes. As López-Hernández puts it, in the case of Madrid universities, the rise of the demand for qualified EFL and CLIL primary teachers in the region brought about by its large-scale bilingual education programmes, "…is evident from the increase in credit load devoted to English and foreign language pedagogy, which is higher than the national average, and which was found to be particularly noticeable in private universities" (2021, p. 146).

This situation has resulted in a new process of revision and renewal of the provision of ITE programmes in Spain. Hence, the critical voices from the universities themselves who called for better academic programmes have been recognised (Custodio Espinar, 2019). Besides, Jover et al. (2016) claim for a more effective strategic plan in the higher education institutions likely to develop both foreign language teaching and CLIL teaching competences in all potential CLIL teachers (López-Hernández, 2021) to overcome the CLIL teacher paradox described by Custodio-Espinar and García Ramos (2020). As a result of this, there are initiatives to make higher education more meaningful for the labour market such as the inclusion of "collaboration and international networking as the bone of the university experience, both for students and teachers" (Piquer Vives & Lorenzo Galés, 2015), the design of the academic programme of education degrees based on current teaching profiles required at bilingual schools (Fernández & Johnson, 2016), the promotion of a relationship between university professors and experienced teachers of bilingual schools (Delicado & Pavón, 2016), the use of team teaching to teach a course on CLIL (Buckingham et al., 2018), or the development of an interdisciplinary approach to initial teacher education (Pérez-Murillo, 2019).

6.1.2 Postgraduate offer to cater for CLIL education

Martín del Pozo (2015) affirms that the consideration of "CLIL teacher training as a specific postgraduate qualification and not only as a complementary one has resulted in a tendency among universities to offer this type of postgraduate specialization courses" (p. 157). The heterogenous and shallow itineraries provided by universities to prepare future teachers for bilingual education scenarios have generated a wide variety of postgraduate programmes that offer the specialisation for this model of education based on CLIL. Tab. 4 offers a summary of the university master's degrees in bilingual education that can be taken in Spain, public and private universities, onsite, blended and online.

Tab. 4: Master's degrees in bilingual education in Spain

Type	Modality	University	Status	Title
Official	Onsite	Universidad Rey Juan Carlos	Public	*Máster Universitario en Enseñanza Bilingüe en Centros Educativos de Educación Primaria e Inmersión en Lengua Inglesa*
Official	Onsite	Universidad Católica de Murcia	Private	*Máster Universitario en Enseñanza Bilingüe: Inglés*
Official	Blended	Universidad CEU Cardenal Herrera	Private	*Máster Universitario en Educación Bilingüe. Inglés y Español*
Official	Blended	Universidad de Extremadura	Public	*Máster Universitario en Enseñanza Bilingüe para Educación Primaria y Secundaria*
Official	Blended	Universidad Nebrija	Private	*Máster Universitario en Enseñanza Bilingüe*
Official	Blended	Universidad Pablo de Olavide	Public	*Máster Universitario en Enseñanza Bilingüe*
Official	Blended	Universidad de Oviedo	Public	*Máster Universitario en Enseñanza Integrada de Lengua Inglesa y Contenidos: Educación Infantil y Primaria*
Official	Online	Universidad de Jaen	Public	*Máster Interuniversitario en Enseñanza Bilingüe y Aprendizaje Integrado de Contenidos y Lenguas Extranjeras*
Official	Online	UNIR	Private	*Máster Universitario en Educación Bilingüe*
Official	Online	Universidad Internacional de Valencia	Private	*Máster Universitario en Educación Bilingüe*

Official	Online	Universidad Francisco de Vitoria	Private	*Máster Universitario en Enseñanza Bilingue*/Bilingual Education
Non-official	Onsite	Universidad Camilo José Cela	Private	*Máster Universitario en Educación Internacional y Bilingüismo*
Non-official	Blended	Universidad de Alcalá	Public	*Máster Universitario en* Bilingual and Multicultural Education
Non-official	Blended	Universidad de la Laguna	Public	*Máster Universitario en Educación Bilingüe*
Non-official	Blended	Universidad de Salamanca	Public	*Máster Universitario en Educación Bilingüe*
Non-official	Blended	Universidad Europea	Private	*Máster Universitario en Educación Bilingüe*
Non-official	Online	Universidad Camilo José Cela	Private	*Máster Universitario en Educación Internacional y Bilingüismo*

Source: Adapted from EB Asociación Enseñanza Bilingüe (2022, Febrero 19). Másteres en enseñanza bilingüe. https://www.ebspain.es/index.php/blog/321-masteres-ensenanza-bilingues

Despite the extensive offer, it is remarkable that nine out of the seventeen masters described are private, and a majority of them are online. All in all, this strategy of postgraduate specialisation does not guarantee that all potential CLIL teachers are prepared for CLIL, and it can be an inhibiting factor for some graduate teachers who want to become effective CLL teachers.

6.2. Meeting the challenges of prospective CLIL teachers: The need for a multivariate analysis

According to Pérez-Cañado (2018), teacher training is a key area for CLIL sustainability. This author offers an analysis of teacher training needs and challenges from multifaceted perspectives based on the description of the CLIL teacher profile and how the latest investigation reveals advances and shortcomings in attaining the desired profile she describes. Based on her meta-analysis, Tab. 5 offers a synthesis of the challenges from the point of view of prospective teachers and how the proposals presented can match them.

Tab. 5: Prospective CLIL teacher training: Challenges and proposals

	CLIL teacher profile	Challenges	Proposals
Key Com- petence	Linguistic and intercultural	Still need for further linguistic training	Promoting plurilingualism at universities Creating bilingual degrees taught through EMI
	Pedagog- ical and organisational	Provide specific CLIL methodological training in under- graduate degrees	Modifying existing undergraduate degrees Incorporating specific contents on CLIL in existing courses Fostering internships in bilingual schools
	Interper- sonal and collaborative	Increase collaboration Attention to diversity	Promoting collaborative action research Ongoing research on specific areas
	Scientific knowledge	Geographical diffe- rences found in pre- service CLIL teachers	Learning from the good practices (European teachers) Reinforcing CLIL preparation in university teacher trainers
	Reflective and developmental	Lack of knowledge on the effects and functioning of CLIL in evidence-based research Lack of participation in MA degrees, ex- change programmes and courses on CLIL	Promoting research strands re- lated to bilingual education in end of degree dissertations

Source: Adapted from Pérez-Cañado (2018)

This strategy of designing proposals based on challenges, which has a propae-deutic character, can palliate the heterogenous panorama caused by the lack of proper CLIL teacher education and training.

Moreover, it is also necessary to consider specific training needs of future po-tential CLIL teachers depending on the type of teacher they are (i.e., language teacher, content teacher), the levels they work at (i.e., pre-primary, primary, secondary, university teacher), and the different contexts they are in (i.e., state, semi-private, private schools or universities). Fig. 13 shows how these variables affect CLIL teacher preparation.

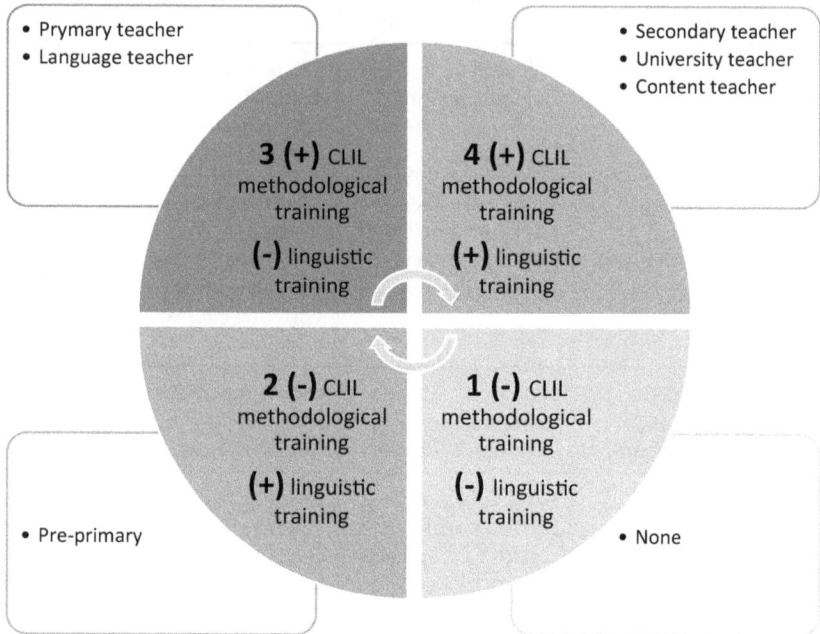

- Prymary teacher
- Language teacher

- Secondary teacher
- University teacher
- Content teacher

3 (+) CLIL methodological training

(-) linguistic training

4 (+) CLIL methodological training

(+) linguistic training

2 (-) CLIL methodological training

(+) linguistic training

1 (-) CLIL methodological training

(-) linguistic training

- Pre-primary

- None

Fig. 13: CLIL teacher education according to the type of teacher and the level

It is clear that language teachers, who already include in their training the teaching and learning of the foreign language, need additional CLIL methodological training. On the other hand, content teachers, who master the scientific knowledge but not the pedagogy of teaching this content in bilingual contexts nor the guarantee of having learnt a foreign language in their degree programmes, need a balanced training in both aspects of CLIL teacher education.

From the point of view of the level of the teacher, pre-primary teacher education for CLIL should put the emphasis on language training since there is scientific evidence of how infants are more likely to learn better the oral skills of the foreign language such as pronunciation (Custodio-Espinar, 2021). Besides, the methodological training provided in their degree is itself in harmony with the principles and theories behind CLIL (i.e., active methodologies, global and cross-curricular approach to learning, learner-centred methodologies, or interaction). As for the CLIL primary teachers, they have the challenge to help students build up scientific learning of specific curricular content in the foreign language. Therefore, they need preparation to understand the underpinnings of bilingual education in order to ensure content learning at a similar level as the one performed by students in non-bilingual schools.

In this sense, Custodio Espinar and García Ramos (2020) confirm, in line with previous studies, that "the level of English is directly related to the global level of methodological competence in CLIL, since level C2 presents differences with levels B2 and C1 in the main dependent variable, in favour of C2 with an effect size of 3%" (p. 21). However, no differences are found between levels B2 and C1 in their competence to plan CLIL lessons, which is explained by the type of accreditation that primary teachers enjoyed at the beginning of the implementation of the Bilingual Programme of the Community of Madrid. This process that combined teacher linguistic and methodological training accredited teachers holding a B2 level to participate in the programme. Notwithstanding the lower level in the foreign language of this group of teachers, they demonstrated a high competence to plan CLIL lessons with no statistical differences found with the teachers who have a C1 level, which suggests that the focus of primary teacher education should be primarily on the principles and the methodology of CLIL education. Finally, the gradual specialisation of the content learnt at secondary education and at university in combination with the learning of a foreign language requires a more balanced training of the academic language of the content and the pedagogy necessary to teach that content (Shulman, 2015) and to do it in CLIL.

All in all, as Wolff (2012) puts it, "CLIL teacher education, if taken seriously, constitutes a fundamental part of all teacher education, that every teacher should be educated, in fact, as a CLIL teacher" (p. 107), thus no prospective CLIL teacher should be in quadrant 1 with low English and methodological training, and no differences as the ones portraited by López Hernández (2021) between private and state universities should exist.

6.3 Context analysis of preservice CLIL teacher education in different countries: The case of Spain, USA and Japan

So far, the education context described in this work suggests that CLIL teachers should be prepared to meet the needs of a diverse, global and pluricultural and plurilinguistic classroom. In the case of Spain, Custodio Espinar (2019) offers the following summary, based on MECD (2013, pp. 317–318), of how preservice primary and secondary teachers are prepared. Primary teachers study a 4-year degree in primary education (240 ECTS) and have teaching practice at schools every year (50 ECTS, including the practicum and the dissertation). There is the possibility to study *menciones* (mentions), a type of specialisation with a very low ECTS value (30–60 ECTS). The mentions were offered by universities in consonance with the Royal Decree 1594/2011, of November 4, which establishes the teaching specialties of Infant and Primary teachers. They are:

- Educación Infantil (Infant Education).
- Educación Primaria (Primary Education).
- Lengua extranjera: Inglés (Foreign Language: English).
- Lengua extranjera: Francés (Foreign Language: French).
- Educación Física (Physical Education).
- Música (Music).
- Pedagogía Terapéutica (Therapeutic Pedagogy).
- Audición y Lenguaje (Hearing and Speech).

This means that the specialisation to teach a foreign language relies in one mention of 30–60 ECTS. In addition, a B1 level in a foreign language is compulsory to complete the degree (B2 for the mention in a foreign language). García Jiménez and Lorente García (2014) point out that a generalist perspective has been chosen in this academic programme, with the mentions substituting the old elective subjects (*asignaturas optativas*) and relegating the specialisation for postgraduate studies.

As for the secondary teachers, they have to study a 4-year degree in specific content areas after which they have to complete a master's degree in Teaching in Secondary Schools (60 ECTS; regulated by law), which involves a practicum of 16 ECTS (including the master's dissertation), an average of 360 hours of internship at schools, depending on the university, which represents 20 % of the total of the master's degree.

Some of the universities that offer these degrees include specific training for CLIL in their academic programmes, mainly the private ones (López Hernández, 2021), which has resulted in a heterogeneous preparation of undergraduate and postgraduate prospective CLIL teachers.

As for Japan, where CLIL has been introduced as a solution to improve EFL teaching practices (Ikeda, 2021), it is necessary to look at the national curriculum called the Course of Study, ELT, and the ELT teacher education system. According to Sasajima (2019) English has been taught only in secondary education since 1945 until 2020, when it was introduced in primary education too. The Japanese curriculum is, according to the author, "a rigid curriculum comprising accurate English language skills (listening, reading, speaking, and writing), the grammar syllabus and vocabulary size, although apparently referring to com-municative language teaching (CLT)" (p. 289). Besides, the flexible credit-based teacher education system does not foster English teaching and learning prepa-ration "since the programs only include a three-week teaching practicum and minimal course requirements in terms of ELT (English literature, English lin-guistics, English communication, and English cross-cultural understanding)" (p. 290). As a result, English teachers are not fully prepared to face the challenges of CLIL education because they even lack the knowledge of ELT methodology (Sasajima, 2019).

The need for bilingual education and teacher preparation for it is totally dif-ferent in the USA, where, according to Spies et al. (2017), "by the 2030s, 40% of the US school population in general will be children who speak a language other than English in the home (Aud et al., 2012; Magruder, Hayslip, Espinosa, & Matera, 2013)" (pp. 23–24). In this context, appropriate bilingual education programmes are key to language and literacy development of young children who are dual language learners (DLL) since an early stage in education (Spies et al., 2017). However, it is noteworthy that, despite the figures of the increasing population of DLL, an inadequate preparation for teachers in the development and implementation of these programmes is still a reality (Spies, 2017; Zepeda et al., 2011).

An interesting aspect of comparing teacher training for bilingual education is to look at the competencies or standards they are supposed to acquire. Zepeda et al. (2011, p. 11) include among these competences:

- understanding the complexities in first and second language and literacy development;
- the relationships between culture and language development, including iden-tity issues;
- specific pedagogical strategies to support the development of English;
- the use of appropriate resource materials;
- understanding appropriate and authentic assessment for DLL populations;
- and the development of professionalism (p. 11)

This set of standards that is the reference for quality professional preparation of DLL teachers is similar to Pérez Cañado's CLIL teacher competencies list (2017). But more importantly, both frameworks are key to successful training of bilin-gual education teachers since they are clearly related to students' academic per-formance (Zepeda et al., 2011) in bilingual contexts whether CLIL, ELT or dual education.

This analysis of prospective bilingual teacher education from an international perspective has revealed that (1) initial teacher education for CLIL is still a pending issue, (2) teacher education programmes to cater for bilingual education have to move from theory to practice, and (3) they have to be reformed in accordance with scientific research of the actual needs of bilingual education contexts in which teachers and students are supposed to teach and learn in a language other than their mother tongue. The chapter provided examples and proposals likely to improve the training of prospective CLIL teachers in different bilingual contexts, considering different variables such as the educational stage and their level of specialisation in the language and the content.

Bibliography

Ball, P., Clegg, J., & Kelly, K. (2015). *Putting CLIL into practice*. Oxford University Press.

Bentley, K. (2010). *The TKT (teaching knowledge test) course. CLIL module content and language integrated learning*. Cambridge University Press.

Bertaux, P., Coonan, C. M., Frigols-Martín, M. J., & Mehisto, P. (2010). *The CLIL teacher's competences grid*. Common constitution and language learning (CCLL) Comenius Network.

Buckingham, L. R., Custodio Espinar M., & López Hernández, A. (2018). Collaborative competence in pre-service teacher training: A team-teaching experience, presented at *IV Congreso internacional sobre educación bilingüe en un mundo globalizado. Enfoques contemporáneos de enseñanza y aprendizaje*, Comunidad de Madrid and Franklin Institute, Alcalá de Henares, Madrid.

Coyle, D., Hood, P., & Marsh, D. (2010). *CLIL – Content and language integrated learning*. Cambridge University Press.

Custodio Espinar, M. (2019). CLIL teacher education in Spain. In K. Tsuchiya & Pérez-Murillo (Eds.), *Content and language integrated learning in Spanish and Japanese contexts* (pp. 313–337). Cham: Palgrave Macmillan.

Custodio Espinar, M. (2021). La edad, factor de éxito en la adquisición y aprendizaje de la lengua extranjera: ¿mito o realidad? In E. Nieto Moreno de Diezmas (Ed.), *Mitos en torno al aprendizaje de idiomas: generando una opinión crítica a través de la divulgación de investigaciones recientes* (pp. 15–26). Ministerio de Educación y Formación Profesional.

Custodio Espinar, M., & García Ramos, J. (2019). Medida de la competencia para programar AICLE y diagnóstico de las necesidades de formación docente. *Bordón. Revista de Pedagogía, 72*(1), 31–48. https://doi.org/10.13042/Bordon.2019.72250

Custodio-Espinar, M., & García-Ramos, J. M. (2020). Are accredited teachers equally trained for CLIL? The CLIL teacher paradox. *Porta Linguarum*, *33*(1), 9–25.

Dale, L., & Tanner, R. (2012). *CLIL Activities. A resource for subject and language teachers.* Cambridge University Press.

Delicado, G., & Pavón, V. (2016). Training primary student teachers for CLIL: Innovation through collaboration. *Pulso. Revista de Educación*, *39*, 35–57.

European Commission/EACEA/Eurydice. (2020). *The European higher education area in 2020: Bologna process implementation report.* Publications Office of the European Union.

European Higher Education Area (EHEA). (2022, February 19). *Terms of reference of working group on learning and teaching.* Working Group on Learning & Teaching. http://www.ehea.info/Upload/WG_L&T_PT_AD_TORs%20 (2).pdf

Fernández, R., & Johnson, M. (Coords) (2016). *Enseñanza bilingüe en la educación universitaria. El enfoque CLIL del Centro Universitario Cardenal Cisneros.* CUCC.

Ikeda, M., Izumi, S., Watanabe, Y., Pinner, R., & Davis, M. (2021). *Soft CLIL and English language teaching: Understanding Japanese policy, practice and implications.* Routledge.

Jover, G., Fleta, T., & González, R. (2016). La formación inicial de los maestros de educación primaria en el contexto de la enseñanza bilingüe en lengua extranjera. *Bordón. Revista de Pedagogía*, *68*(2), 121–135. https://doi.org/10.13042/ Bordon.2016.68208

López-Hernández, A. (2021). Initial teacher education of primary English and CLIL teachers: An analysis of the training curricula in the universities of the Madrid Autonomous Community (Spain). *International Journal of Learning, Teaching and Educational Research*, *20*(3), 132–150. https://doi.org/10.26803/ ijlter.20.3.9

Marsh, D., Mehisto, P., Wolff, D., & Frigols, M. J. (2010). *European framework for CLIL teacher education: A framework for the professional development of CLIL Teachers.* European Centre for Modern Languages.

Martín del Pozo, M. A. (2013). Formación del profesorado universitario para la docencia en inglés. *Revista de Docencia Universitaria*, *11*(3), 197–218. https:// doi.org/10.4995/redu.2013.5526

Mehisto, P., Marsh, D., & Frigols, M. J. (2008). *Uncovering CLIL: Content and language integrated learning in bilingual and multilingual education.* Macmillan Education.

Pavón, V., & Gaustad, M. (2013). Designing bilingual programmes for higher education in Spain: Organizational, curricular and methodological decisions. *International CLIL Research Journal*, *1*(5), 82–94.

Pérez Cañado, M. L. (2017). CLIL teacher education: Where do we stand and where do we need to go? In *Educación Bilingüe: tendencias educativas y conceptos claves* (pp. 129–144). Ministerio de Educación Cultura y Deporte.

Perez Canado, M. L. (2018). Innovations and challenges in CLIL teacher training. *Theory Into Practice*, *57*(3), 212–221. https://doi.org/10.1080/00405 841.2018.1492238

Pérez Murillo, M. D. (2019). The internationalization of Spanish higher education: An interdisciplinary approach to initial teacher education for CLIL. In K. Tsuchiya & Pérez-Murillo (Eds.), *Content and language integrated learning in Spanish and Japanese contexts* (pp. 339–371). Cham: Palgrave Macmillan.

Piquer Vives, I., & Lorenzo Galés, N. (2015). Reflecting on CLIL innovation. An interview with Do Coyle and Elisabet Pladevall. *Bellaterra Journal of Teaching & Learning Language & Literature*, *8*(1), 86–93. http://dx.doi.org/10.5565/rev/jtl3.610

Sasajima, S. (2019). Teacher development: J-CLIL. In K. Tsuchiya & Pérez-Murillo (Eds.), *Content and language integrated learning in Spanish and Japanese contexts* (pp. 287–312). Cham: Palgrave Macmillan.

Shulman, L. S. (2015). PCK: Its genesis and exodus. In A. Berry, P. Friedrichsen, & J. Loughran (Eds.), *Re-examining pedagogical content knowledge in science education* (pp. 13–23). Routledge.

Smit, U., & Dafouz, E. (2012). Integrating content and language in higher education: An introduction to English-medium policies, conceptual issues and research practices across Europe. *Aila Review*, *25*(1), 1–12.

Spain. Order ECI/3857/2007, 27th of December, that establishes the requirements for the recognition of official university degrees that serve as qualification for working as a teacher of primary education. *Boletín Oficial del Estado* (Official State Bulletin), No. 312, 27th of December 2007. https://www.boe.es/eli/es/o/2007/12/27/eci3857

Spies, T. G., Lyons, C., Huerta, M., Garza, T., & Reding, C. (2017). Beyond professional development: Factors influencing early childhood educators' beliefs and practices working with dual language learners. *Catesol Journal*, *29*(1), 23–50.

Wolff, D. (2012). The European framework for CLIL teacher education. *Synergies Italie*, 8, 105–116.

Zepeda, M., Castro, D. C., & Cronin, S. (2011). Preparing early childhood teachers to work with young dual language learners. *Child Development Perspectives, 5,* 10–14. https://doi.org/10.1111/j.1750-8606.2010.00141.x

Chapter 7. Inservice teacher training: Contentious issues and pending tasks

Abstract: The issue of teacher training has been systematically studied on an international scale in TALIS reports (TALIS 2008, 2013, 2018), which have shown that providing quality initial and continuous training is one of the main takeaways. Thus, if teacher training is essential in mainstream education, all the more reason why quality CLIL provisions need to be built around solid inservice teacher training programmes. The first step in CLIL training for inservice teachers is to define what, when and how to be trained. In addition, in the context of inservice CLIL teacher training, there are inhibiting factors that prevent teachers from participating in the training programmes available for them. This generates a heterogenous panorama concerning teachers' competence profile that depends on the wide variety of training actions taken by the different CLIL teachers. However, far from being a problem, this complex scenario can be an excellent source of training activities that merge the practical experience shared among teachers. This symbiotic relationship between the training actions and their transferability should guide the search of high-need areas of training for CLIL teachers. Custodio-Espinar and García-Ramos (2019, 2020), Hillyard (2011), Madrid and Julius (2017), Marsh et al. (2015), Pérez-Cañado (2018), Sasajima (2019), or Tsui (2020) among others have highlighted some of these areas and key factors.This chapter includes a thorough analysis of training policies and actual training needs and priorities perceived by inservice CLIL teachers from an international perspective. The result of this analysis can serve as a reference for the design of training strategies and programmes likely to promote inservice training and to improve the classroom practice of CLIL teachers across continents. Some examples of good practices from different contexts are provided as an inspiration and recognition of the efforts made by teachers and CLIL associations so far in this field.

Keywords: Bilingual education, inservice training, teacher qualifications, professional development, training courses.

7.1 Conceptualising and defining CLIL teacher training: The "problem" of heterogeneity of profiles and backgrounds

As Andreas Schleicher affirms in the foreword of Talis 2018 report, "society no longer rewards students just for what they know – Google knows everything – but for what they can do with what they know. Today's teachers need to help students think for themselves, work with others, and develop identity, agency and purpose" (OECD, 2019). However, education reforms are usually based on the needs and interests of systems rather than learners, which leads to contradictions. For example, in Japan, where there is a rigid ELT curriculum including recommendations for a communicative approach, the complex teacher culture of the country makes it very difficult for teachers to change their methods (Sasajima, 2019). The report (OECD, 2019) also signals that, apart from content and pedagogy,

> …teachers' formal education and training tends to include instruction on student behaviour and classroom management (for 72% of all teachers across OECD countries and economies in TALIS), monitoring students' development and learning (70%), teaching cross-curricular skills (65%), teaching in a mixed-ability setting (62%) and use of information and communication technology (ICT) for teaching (56%). (OECD, 2019)

However, only 35% refers to teaching in a multicultural or multilingual setting as an element of teachers' formal education or training. This reinforces the contradiction between policies like the plurilingual policy of the European Union (EU) (see Chapter 1) and practices both in initial education programmes, which generally lack provision for this type of educational contexts (see Chapter 6), and in the design of inservice training programmes, which seem to put the emphasis on other aspects of teachers' development.

In this scenario, lifelong learning, mainly based on out-of-school types of training such as attending courses or seminars, is to palliate the deficiencies. According to OECD (2019), 70 % of the total training actions are this type, which clearly moves away from alternative training proposals with a greater potential for transferability. Interesting alternative proposals are the ones described in Banegas et al. (2013), who used action research, in Sasajima (2019), who describes the benefits of lesson study in teacher training or the proposal by Banegas and del Pozo Beamud (2020), who suggest the use of ethnographic studies to improve the quality of CLIL teacher education and training. In line with these alternative forms of training, it is interesting to note the change of perspective towards teacher education presented by the new editors of the Asia-Pacific Journal of

Teacher Education (Biesta et al., 2020), who include, among their eight challenges for teacher education research, the importance of investigating how national and transnational organisations intersect with teacher education reforms, and how they are resisted and recontextualised by networks of educators and schools implementing bottom-up teacher education initiatives and programmes. A clear example of this is the Japan CLIL Pedagogy Association (J-CLIL) that will be described below.

It is also remarkable that, contrary to TALIS (2018) report, in which more than 80 % of teachers affirmed that their training had a positive impact on their teaching practices, Pérez Cañado (2016) had already signalled that traditional training actions do not always catch up with the expectations nor have the necessary impact on CLIL teacher expertise to impart bilingual education. Besides, some of these training actions, such as exchange programmes, or linguistic and methodology courses abroad, are not often taken by teachers (Lancaster, 2016; Milla Lara & Casas Pedrosa, 2018) and "although there are more and more academic events such as courses, seminars, and workshops, among others, that are organized by different institutions, they do not seem to satisfy the teachers' needs yet" (Milla Lara & Casas Pedrosa, 2018, p. 176). Pérez Cañado (2016) also pointed out that teacher training should be a priority in the process of preparation of CLIL models in Europe. The author identified as major issues the lack of training in the foreign language, the knowledge of the CLIL approach and the necessary methodologies to develop it in practice, which refer to the specific dual training required by CLIL teachers, but the main weaknesses systematically identified in the literature (Milla Lara & Casas Pedrosa, 2018).

This lack of training of inservice CLIL teachers is perpetuated by the accreditation system and subsequent voluntary participation in CLIL training activities, which was coined by Custodio-Espinar and García Ramos (2019) as "the CLIL teacher paradox", in reference to the so-called "CLIL teacher" who has never received any type of CLIL training. As De la Maya Retamar and Luengo González (2015) put it, "we are not preparing our students in line with what the new school system demands" (p. 118). This involves that "teachers need training not undertaken earlier in their careers, in order to participate in plurilingual programs" (Madrid, 2010, cited in De la Maya Retamar & Luegno González, 2015, p. 118). If we add to this that the accreditation systems designed do not always take into account methodological training in CLIL, and that inservice teacher training in CLIL is not mandatory, this lack of pre-while-post training has resulted in a wide diversity of CLIL teacher profiles ranging from CLIL teachers with no CLIL training to hyper-trained CLIL teachers who still feel the need for training (Custodio Espinar, 2019).

These differences in the CLIL teacher profile portray the variety of itineraries designed for CLIL teacher education, training and accreditation across Europe. Almenta (2011) offered a critical evaluation, based on Eurydice report 2006 (European Commission, 2006), concluding that at that time there were many different options to consider CLIL in teaching qualification such as classes or courses in Austria, bilingual/international degrees in England and the Netherlands, a certificate of bilingual education and immersion in Northern Ireland, special further qualification for bilingual education in German, a certificate for teaching NLA (non-linguistic areas) in a foreign language in France, initial training for CLIL in the other official language or in a foreign language in Finland, optional modules and postgraduate studies in CLIL in Spain, or specialisation in a second subject or a linguistic area and a foreign language in Poland. Big differences were also appreciated when comparing inservice training provision in the different European regions. Some examples are CLIL teaching pilot experiments in Belgium, training actions based on international cooperation agreements with institutions such as *Goethe Ins*titut or *Alliance Française* in Czech Republic, Latvian National Agencies for Language Training that offer courses in bilingual teaching methodology, experienced teachers who act as trainers of new teachers in Sweden and CLIL courses and language courses in Spain or abroad provided by Teacher's Training Centres. However, as Almenta (2011) remarks, only Italy, the Netherlands, Austria and Finland (in the case of CLIL with a foreign language) strongly recommend inservice training for CLIL. In a majority of the countries it is not mandatory nor a requirement for CLIL teaching.

A more recent description of the qualifications needed to teach a non-language subject in a foreign language was included in Eurydice 2017 (European Commission, 2017). According to it, teachers need

- to have a very good knowledge both of the subject taught and the language in which it is taught
- to be familiar with the requirements of CLIL methodology
- some education systems require that foreign language teachers hold a qualification in both foreign languages and a non-language subject (p. 91)

However, not all countries regulate specific qualifications for CLIL and, in those that they exist, they usually refer to the level required in the target language of teachers who are not qualified as foreign language teachers. The minimum level in a majority of countries varies from B2 to C1 according to the Common European Framework of Reference for Languages (CEFRL) (Council of Europe, 2001) and some countries also ask for specific language certificates/examinations. Fig. 14 describes the qualifications required at the central level to work in schools providing CLIL (Type A, in which subjects are taught in the language of schooling and some subjects in a foreign language) instruction in primary and/ or general secondary education in the school year 2015/2016.

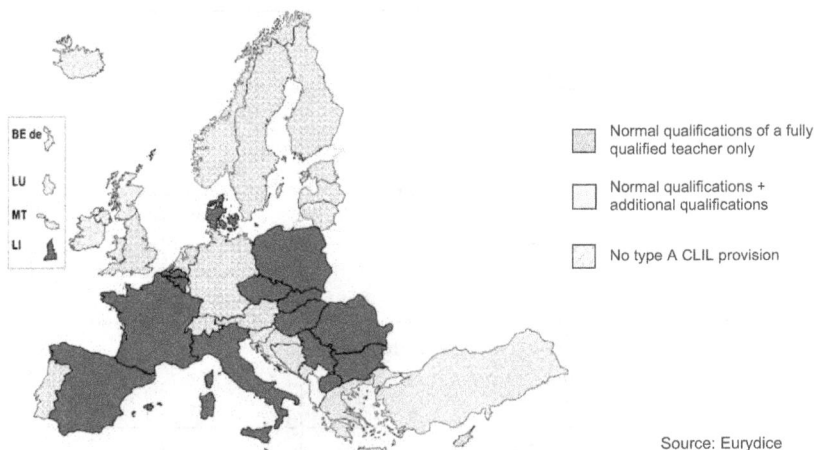

Fig. 14: Qualifications required to work in schools providing CLIL instruction in primary and/or general secondary education in the school year 2015/16. Source: Eurydice (European Commission, 2017, p. 92)

Countries in blue pattern (Portugal, Germany, or Finland) require normal qualifications of a fully qualified teacher only; countries in red (Spain, France, or Italy) also ask for additional qualifications and the rest of countries do not offer CLIL Type A provision (European Commission, 2017). A description of the additional qualifications required is shown in Tab. 6.

Tab. 6: Additional qualifications required to impart CLIL Type A

Countries	Linguistic certification*	CLIL education/training
Liechtenstein	C2 level	---
Belgium (Flemish) Czech Republic	C1 level	---
Italy	C1 level	One-year university course in CLIL (60 credits)

Spain	B2-C1 level	Some autonomous communities training in CLIL
Serbia	From B1 to C1 levels	---
Bulgaria Poland	B2 level	---
Former Yugoslav Republic of Macedonia	B1 level	---
Slovakia	State Language Examination	---
Romania	---	Course/seminar on CLIL methodology
Belgium (French) Denmark France	Qualifications or examination Bachelor's degree in the TL	---
Hungary	Full qualifications as a foreign language teacher; and in a specific non-language subject	---

*Usually applies to teachers who do not hold an academic degree in the target language

Source: Adapted from (European Commission, 2017, pp. 92–93).

Only three of the thirteen countries in which additional qualifications are needed to impart CLIL require specific methodological training in CLIL, and in the case of Spain, only in some regions. From a critical approach to this scenario, Martín del Pozo (2015) suggests the following directions to compensate the balance between linguistic and methodological training of CLIL teachers: (1) Shift attention from language level to language type required; (2) Methodological awareness. This would include teaching practice in their native language. A CLIL course is suggested in response to the challenge posed to teachers by CLIL practice (p. 165). These contentious issues are still pending in the CLIL teacher training agenda since, as Martin del Pozo says, there is no agreement of competences and qualifications needed for teachers to join a CLIL programme (2015).

Moreover, at the base of the problem is the fact that the training offer does not reach the entire target population. According to TALIS 18 the "participation in training actions is restricted by schedule conflicts and lack of incentives to engage in these activities" (OECD, 2019). All in all, different teachers need different areas of training in different ways and times and it is impossible to design courses that fit all sizes. Besides, in words of Lozano Martínez (2017), there is no consensus among teachers themselves about some of the challenges that must be faced in a bilingual programme such as training (p. 93).

7.2 The design of training courses on CLIL: Pre-while-post CLILing

According to TALIS 2018 results, these are the key factors reported by teachers that should lead policy intervention: (1) reducing class sizes (reported by 65 % of teachers); (2) improving teacher salaries (64 %); (3) offering high-quality professional development for teachers (55 %); and (4) reducing teachers' administration load (55 %) (OECD, 2019). Concerning the content of the training actions, these are the main areas of training, which enjoy an increasing demand: "advanced information and communication technology (ICT) skills, teaching methods for multicultural/multilingual settings and teaching methods for students with special needs" (OECD, 2019). These high-need areas of training for teachers in general are applicable to CLIL teachers in particular (Madrid & Pérez Cañado, 2018; Pérez-Cañado, 2016).

From the point of view of student teachers and their professors, Madrid and Julius (2017) have also identified key factors in bilingual education at university level (Tab. 7).

Tab. 7: Key factors in bilingual education at university level

Area	Factors
Language	Teacher/professor linguistic preparation and L2 level
	Speaking clearly to students in class at an intelligible volume
	Proper pronunciation and oral expression in class
	Language exchanges with native speakers
	Living in in English-Speaking Countries
	Achieving a B2 level or higher in English
	Consistent feedback from the students to ensure content comprehension and detect confusion or false impressions

Method-ology	Emphasis on interactive activities and oral communication
	Didactic preparation in CLIL
	Content Preparation
	Working with tasks and projects related to everyday life
	Individual work
	Variety of exercises and activities
	Availability of materials and human resources
	Cooperative work
	Implementation of integrated content and language projects
	Audiovisual materials
	Professional development and continuing education
Motivation	Teacher/professor motivation and personal commitment to the programme
	Students' personal motivation and interest in the programme
	Motivating students in class by highlighting successes and downplaying mistakes

Source: Adapted from Madrid and Julius (2017, p. 59)

Considering these areas and factors, the ideal route for an adequate training of CLIL teachers should include three fundamental phases. A first phase, in which potential CLIL teachers can learn about the pillars of CLIL and the methodological principles underpinning effective CLIL lessons. In a second phase, these teachers should be able to observe and experience CLIL practices in a controlled and safe environment. Finally, once they start working in bilingual programmes, they need to keep on receiving training in specific areas of this eclectic approach, which are likely to improve their particular teaching and learning context. Needless to say that, throughout the three phases, they should have opportunities to improve their foreign language proficiency. Therefore, the training could run from the general to the particular and from theory to practice, in a gradual transition that can guarantee a quality education and training of CLIL teachers (Fig. 15).

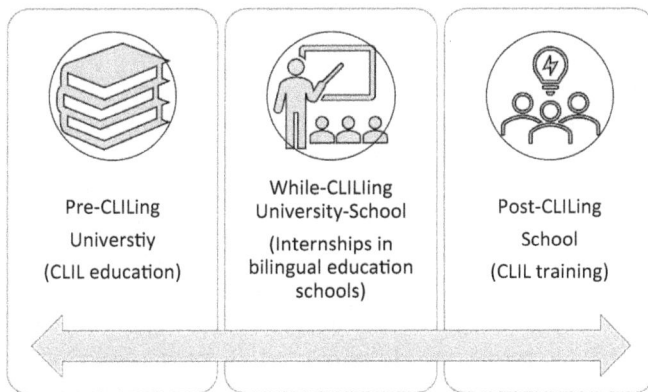

Fig. 15: Ideal route for quality CLIL teacher education and training. Source: Own elaboration

In this continuum, pre-CLILing actions involve the study of courses about bilingual education and CLIL, as well as foreign language courses or courses imparted through a foreign language to improve the language proficiency of students. Academic programmes for potential CLIL teachers should include workshops and seminars about CLIL, or even proper CLIL courses as part of their syllabuses. Some, but not all academic programmes, offer in their education degrees this type of content (López Hernández, 2021; Torres Zúñiga & Carrasco Flores, 2020). After this pre-CLILing introduction, student CLIL teachers and inservice CLIL teachers can relate and exchange knowledge, information, experience, concerns, at schools and both would benefit from this relationship (Custodio Espinar, 2019). The former would have an opportunity to observe the theory into practice before facing a CLIL classroom on their own. The later would be bound to link their experience to the theories of CLIL after years of practice. This while-CLILing stage provides a double track exposure to bilingual education facilitating feedback between theory and practice as the basis for the design and review of academic training plans and lifelong training plans. Finally, once CLIL teachers have developed their own understanding of CLIL, they can benefit from exchanging their good practices, from observing their classrooms, from analysing and assessing their lessons, from leading innovation projects, seminars, training actions at their schools, in a nutshell, from training actions rooted in their contexts.

Unfortunately, there are many CLIL teachers who lack proper pre/while/post training, as described in this chapter. Hence, inservice training is designed to palliate deficiencies rather than to consolidate and reinforce CLIL teacher competencies (Custodio Espinar, 2019), which has led to the heterogenous CLIL teacher profile explained above. However, this scenario can be of extremely importance in the design of inservice training actions if they are based on the collaboration and interrelation of trained and untrained teachers. For example, in Spain, in the Community of Madrid, The *MentorActúa* Programme offers teachers the opportunity to participate in a training activity through school pairing. This collaboration generates a dialogue within the educational community of both schools, providing visibility to good practices and favouring their exchange. The participants thus have the opportunity to visit the schools and classrooms of other teachers in a guided sequence, with the aim of renewing and invigorating pedagogical and methodological change through observation and the exchange of experiences (Comunidad de Madrid, 2021, p. 108). It is paramount to continue expanding training actions based on teacher observation and collaboration between teachers and educational centres as a training modality for the professional development of teachers due to their great potential of transferability. As Tsui (2020) puts it, "it is the development of professional discourse and the collaborative pedagogical enquiry among teachers and teacher educators that would empower teachers to make professional decisions in their local contexts" (p. 31). These type of training is key to the successful homogenisation of the level of competence of inservice teachers in the CLIL approach since it guaranties a multilevel training likely to adapt and suit the particular needs of different CLIL teachers at the same time in a meaningful context for all of them. Besides, it contributes to strengthen the relationship between the different CLIL teachers at school, i.e., content teachers/language teachers; pre-primary/primary/secondary teachers; novel teachers/experienced teachers; untrained teachers/trained teachers; preservice teachers/inservice teachers; soft CLIL teachers/hard CLIL teachers; low language proficiency teachers/high language proficiency teachers, etc. Because, as Banegas and del Pozo Beamud (2020) conclude, "professional development courses need to incorporate teachers' beliefs, past and present practices in context" (p. 257).

Another advantage of this contextualised mode of training is the change of paradigm in teacher training from listening to teachers' voices in the design of teacher training proposals and regulations to develop bilingual education (Lozano Martínez & Chacón Beltrán, 2017; Lozano-Martínez, 2017; Milla Lara & Casas Pedrosa, 2018), to putting the focus on teachers' performance as the core of training actions developed among themselves, including the non-accredited teachers who are not usually participants in CLIL training actions but could benefit from them if they are developed at their schools. The outputs of these collaborative training actions should lead scientific research and inform the educational authorities responsible for the design of bilingual programmes. Because as Vinuesa Benítez and Gisbert Da Cruz (2017) put it, the evaluation of training actions made by teachers should be a key element in the design of the training offer (p. 57) and it is necessary to keep open channels of communication between teachers and their educational administration (Lozano Martínez, 2017).

7.3 Inservice training initiatives in different contexts

Effective teacher training is a common concern all over the world. In the context of bilingual education, it is a key factor that has promoted the creation of different associations that work to guarantee effective bilingual education. Below, three examples from three different contexts are provided.

7.3.1 Asociación "Enseñanza Bilingüe", EB Spain[6]

The website of this association introduces itself as an Observatory of Bilingual Teaching in Spain aiming at ensuring the effective implementation of this type of education in the different bilingual programmes implemented in Spain. The association devotes efforts to collecting and disseminating information and experiences, the exchange of information on bilingual programmes and regulations, the study and analysis of bilingual programmes in Spain, conducting research in the field of bilingual education, the preparation and publication of studies and documents related to bilingual education, participation in forums and debates on bilingual education, and CLIL teacher training. These activities and actions, as well as the organisation of one of the most important international congress in bilingual education and CLIL, are developed in partnership with other national and international associations, administrations and universities (*Asociación Enseñanza Bilingüe*, 2022). This association also offers resources for pre-primary, primary and secondary bilingual education.

7.3.2 National Association for Bilingual Education, NABE[7]

It is the only national professional organisation devoted to representing bilingual/multilingual students and bilingual education professionals in the USA

---

6   https://ebspain.es/
7   https://nabe.org/

(National Association for Bilingual Education, 2022). NABE's mission is to advocate for educational equity and excellence for bilingual/multilingual students in a global society. As EB Spain, with whom they collaborate, NABE organises an annual international conference (the 52nd will be held in Portland, Oregon, next February 2023) and annual symposiums, and provides support for professional development in dual language programmes.

7.3.3 Japan CLIL Pedagogy Association, J-CLIL[8]

This organisation was established in April 2017. They develop several activities such as CLIL study meetings, seminars, journal publishing, materials development, CLIL research networks and other activities to promote CLIL and CBLT (Content-based Language Teaching) pedagogy. J-CLIL also organises study groups, workshops, and lectures in order to promote research and practices for the implementation of CLIL and CBLT in Japan (Japan CLIL Pedagogy Association, 2017). J-CLIL has stablished five branches in western Japan, Tohoku area, Hokuriku, Kyushu and a fifth branch in Taiwan.

These three examples show a common interest in promoting quality bilingual education, which despite their social, economic and linguistic differences, share the design of similar continuous teacher training activities.

Bibliography

Almenta, E. (2011). CLIL teacher training across Europe. Current state of the art, good practices and guidelines for the future. http://uma.academia.edu/Estef aniaAlmenta

Asociación Enseñanza Bilingüe. (2022, March 19). *Presentación.* https://ebspain. es/index.php/asociacion

Banegas, D. L. (2019). Teacher professional development in language-driven CLIL: A case study. *Latin American Journal of Content & Language Integrated Learning, 12*(2), 242–264. https://doi.org/10.5294/laclil.2019.12.2.3

Banegas, D. L., & del Pozo Beamud, M. (2020). Content and language integrated learning: A duoethnographic study about CLIL pre-service teacher education in Argentina and Spain. *RELC Journal, 1,* 14. https://doi.org/10.1177/00336 88220930442

Banegas, D., Pavese, A., Velázquez, A., & Vélez, S. M. (2013). Teacher professional development through collaborative action research: Impact on foreign

---

8   https://www.j-clil.com/english

English-language teaching and learning. *Educational Action Research*, *21*(2), 185–201. https://doi.org/10.1080/09650792.2013.789717

Biesta, G., Takayama, K., Kettle, M., & Heimans, S. (2020). Teacher education between principle, politics, and practice: A statement from the new editors of the Asia-Pacific Journal of Teacher Education. *Asia-Pacific Journal of Teacher Education*, *48*(5), 455–459. https://doi.org/10.1080/1359866X.2020.1818485

Comunidad de Madrid. (2021). *Plan de innovación y formación docente de la Comunidad de Madrid*. Consejería de Educación, Universidad, Ciencia y Portavocía. http://www.madrid.org/bvirtual/BVCM050412.pdf

Council of Europe. (2001). *Common European framework of reference for languages: Learning, teaching, assessment*. Cambridge University Press.

Custodio Espinar, M. (2019). CLIL teacher education in Spain. In K. Tsuchiya & M. D. Pérez Murillo (Eds.), *Content and language integrated learning in Spanish and Japanese contexts* (pp. 313–337). Cham: Palgrave Macmillan.

Custodio Espinar, M., & García Ramos, J. (2019). Medida de la competencia para programar AICLE y diagnóstico de las necesidades de formación docente. *Bordón. Revista de Pedagogía*, *72*(1), 31–48. https://doi.org/10.13042/Bordon.2019.72250

Custodio-Espinar, M., & García-Ramos, J. M. (2020). Are accredited teachers equally trained for CLIL? The CLIL teacher paradox. *Porta Linguarum*, *33*(1), 9–25.

De la Maya Retamar, G., & Luengo González, R. (2015). Teacher training programs and development of plurilingual competence. In M. L. Pérez-Cañado, D. Marsh, & J. Rodríguez Padilla (Eds.), *CLIL in action: Voices from the classroom* (pp. 114–129). Cambridge Scholars Publishing.

European Commission, Directorate-General for Education, Youth, Sport and Culture. (2006). *Content and language integrated learning (CLIL) at school in Europe*. Publications Office.

European Commission/EACEA/Eurydice. (2017). *Key data on teaching languages at school in Europe – 2017 Edition. Eurydice report*. Publications Office. https://data.europa.eu/doi/10.2797/04255

Hillyard, S. (2011). First steps in CLIL: Training the teachers. *Latin American Journal of Content & Language Integrated Learning*, *4*(2), 1–12.

Japan CLIL Pedagogy Association. (2017). *About J-CLIL*. https://www.j-clil.com/english-j-clil

Lancaster, N. K. (2016). Stakeholder perspectives on CLIL in a monolingual context. *English Language Teaching*, *9*(2), 148–177. http://dx.doi.org/10.5539/elt.v9n2p148

López-Hernández, A. (2021). Initial teacher education of primary English and CLIL teachers: An analysis of the training curricula in the universities of the Madrid Autonomous Community (Spain). *International Journal of Learning, Teaching and Educational Research, 20*(3), 132–150. https://doi.org/10.26803/ijlter.20.3.9

Lozano-Martínez, L. (2017). Los docentes en los programas de educación bilingüe en Cantabria. *Estudios de lingüística inglesa aplicada, 17*, 93–123. http://dx.doi.org/10.12795/elia.2017.i17.05

Lozano Martínez, L., & Chacón Beltrán, M. R. (2017). La legislación de los programas bilingües en educación infantil y primaria desde la perspectiva docente. *RAEL: Revista electrónica de lingüística aplicada, 16*(1), 3–22.

Madrid Fernández, D., & Julius, S. M. (2017). Quality factors in bilingual education at the university level. *Porta Linguarum: Revista internacional de didáctica de las lenguas extranjeras, (28)*, 49–66.

Madrid Fernández, D., & Perez Cañado, M. L. (2018). Innovations and challenges in attending to diversity through CLIL. *Theory into Practice, 57*(3), 241–249. https://doi.org/10.1080/00405841.2018.1492237

Marsh, D., Pérez-Cañado, M. L., & Padilla, J. R. (Eds.). (2015). *CLIL in action: Voices from the classroom*. Cambridge Scholars Publishing.

Martín del Pozo, M. A. (2013). Formación del profesorado universitario para la docencia en inglés. *Revista de Docencia Universitaria, 11*(3), 197–218. https://doi.org/10.4995/redu.2013.5526

Milla Lara, M. D., & Casas Pedrosa, A. V. (2018). Teacher perspectives on CLIL implementation: A within-group comparison of key variables. *Porta Linguarum: Revista internacional de didáctica de las lenguas extranjeras, 29*, 159–180.

National Association for Bilingual Education. (2022, March 19). *NABE's mission is to advocate for educational equity and excellence for bilingual/multilingual students in a global society*. https://nabe.org/about-nabe/nabes-mission/

Organization for Economic Co-operation and Development (OECD). (2014). *TALIS 2013 results: An international perspective on teaching and learning*. OECD Publishing. https://doi.org/10.1787/9789264196261-en

Organization for Economic Co-operation and Development (OECD). (2019). *TALIS 2018 results (Volume I): Teachers and school leaders as lifelong learners*. OECD Publishing. https://doi.org/10.1787/1d0bc92a-en

Pérez Cañado, M. L. (2016). Teacher training needs for bilingual education: Inservice teacher perceptions. *International Journal of Bilingual Education and Bilingualism, 19*(3), 266–95. https://doi.org/10.1080/13670050.2014.980778

Pérez Cañado, M. L. (2018). Innovations and challenges in CLIL teacher training. *Theory Into Practice*, *57*(3), 1–10. https://doi.org/10.1080/00405 841.2018.1492238

Sasajima, S. (2019). Teacher development: J-CLIL. In K. Tsuchiya & M. D. Pérez Murillo (Eds.), *Content and language integrated learning in Spanish and Japanese contexts* (pp. 287–312). Cham: Palgrave Macmillan.

Torres Zúñiga, L., & Carrasco Flores, J. A. (2020). La enseñanza del inglés en educación infantil en España: Implicaciones para la formación del profesorado. *Docencia e Investigación: Revista de la Escuela Universitaria de Magisterio de Toledo*, *45*(31), 5–23.

Tsui, A. B. M. (2020). Glocalization and grobalization: Critical issues in English language teaching and teacher education in East Asia. In A. B. Tsui (Ed.), *English language teaching and teacher education in East Asia* (pp. 1–36). Cambridge University Press. https://doi.org/10.1017/9781108856218.002

Virginia Vinuesa Benítez (Dra.) & Xavier Gisbert Da Cruz (2017). Inmersión lingüística para profesores AICOLE. Un Enfoque comunicativo y práctico. *NABE Journal of Research and Practice*, *8*(1), 44–59. https://doi.org/10.1080/ 26390043.2017.12067795